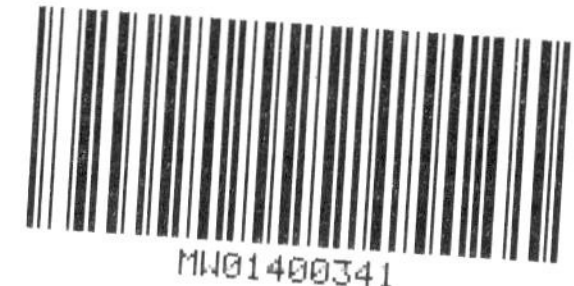

Challenges Galore:
Vocabulary Building Puzzles

BY
ROBERT OLENYCH

ISBN 1-58037-165-5

Printing No. CD-1386

Mark Twain Media, Inc., Publishers
Distributed by Carson-Dellosa Publishing Company, Inc.

Table of Contents

Purpose/Introduction

The purpose of this activity book is to provide teachers and students with a wide range of challenging and motivational vocabulary activities that are different and fun to do. These activities are intended to be used by themselves or to complement existing language programs by providing activities that will require students to work independently or with a partner to problem-solve, learn and apply strategies, think, and have fun.

Since students enjoy solving puzzles and decoding messages, many of the challenges provide the students with an opportunity to do this. Blank templates will be provided for some of the activities to give students the tools they'll need to create their own challenges to share with their classmates.

Most of the challenges have from six to eight activity sheets. As students tackle the first or second sheet, strategies are being developed and the students acquire an understanding of what is expected in each challenge. Similarly, when the activity is taken up, the students may also learn strategies that fellow classmates used to get the answers to some of the questions. As a result, each subsequent challenge becomes that much easier.

These puzzles are vocabulary-building challenges that are presented in a variety of creative and innovative ways. As students work to solve the puzzles and find the hidden messages, they are learning new and often unusual words. The messages found in the Pair of Diamonds activities pertain to special times throughout the year. For example: "Merry Christmas and happy New Year to all." The Combination Puzzle is a multi-task activity because students are required to match up three-letter portions of words to create 12 six-letter words. These words are then used to complete 12 analogous relationships. The Clues Galore and Fewer Clues exercises help students build vocabulary by first coming up with the answers to the clues and then using those clues to reveal a new nine-letter word. Messages in the Zig-Zag Topics puzzles are found by reading down the shaded boxes after students have written in the answers to the clues. The Last Letter-First Letter puzzles are similar to crossword puzzles, except that the last letter of each clue is also the first letter of the next clue. Hidden words are found by taking the letters from the shaded boxes and filling in the message boxes. In the Reveal a Palindrome section students complete several five-letter words and then decode the palindrome sentences. In the Four-Squared puzzles, students write in the answers to clues and then read down or up the shaded boxes to reveal a message. The Back and Forth puzzles challenge students to find six-letter words that fit in the puzzles in a special way. The last three letters of an answer become the first three letters of the next answer and so on. The Acrostic puzzles focus students on finding antonyms and synonyms to words given. Then students must decode the puzzle to find the hidden message. Messages in the Split the Diamond puzzles are found by reading down the shaded boxes after students find the answers to all the clues. Words with specific letter combinations are needed to complete the Word Game puzzles.

Students can be motivated to do just about anything. Once they have worked on a particular kind of activity and have gained some confidence in doing it, some may be ready for a challenge (this is where the blank templates come into play). With encouragement and direction, students can successfully create and share similar challenges with their classmates. Their ability to stick to the task and see it through to completion is very rewarding to the teacher and student alike. Simply seeing the names of their friends on an activity sheet is all the motivation that is required to get others to try their hand at creating an activity.

Teaching Strategies

Getting Started

First:

- make an overhead transparency of an activity
- go over the instructions with the class
- have the class look over the questions and offer possible solutions
- if the answer is correct, print it in the given space
- if difficulties are encountered, isolate key words in the clues
- go to a dictionary, CD-ROM, or other reference materials
- use a thesaurus
- involve the parents or older siblings as a resource only

Second:

- go over the instructions with the class
- permit the students to pursue this activity independently or with a partner
- by brainstorming and by working as a team, students develop and/or share strategies with their partners

Third:

- allow the class to experience the activity after it has been explained
- after a ten-minute time period, stop the class and discuss what has been achieved so far
- if necessary, provide additional clues or strategies to help them in their task
- a specific clue may be addressed, and through a cooperative effort, the class may come up with the answer
- class resumes the activity

Last:

- since each class is made up of students of varying abilities, the same activity can be distributed to the entire group; however, it is important to adjust your expectations accordingly
- some students may be expected to complete at least 80% of the activity, whereas some may only do about half

Time Lines

- many of these activities can be assigned with longer times
- the Pair of Diamonds puzzles, for example, could have a time line of one week
- try to encourage daily time management
- students can be given some class time to work on the activity
- suggest that the students spend 10–15 (quality) minutes on their task at home

Teaching Strategies (continued)

- if specific difficulties are encountered, they can discuss them with a friend or approach the teacher
- anxiety level is reduced
- have the students write "spend 10–15 minutes per night" across the top of the activity
- have the students record the due date at the top
- have the parent(s) sign the worksheet as acknowledgment that they have been made aware of this assignment
- the parents can now work with the teacher in encouraging their children to work toward achieving specific goals

Taking It Up

First:

- before correcting the activity, ask the class which of the questions proved to be rather difficult
- if a fair number of students had difficulty with the same question or clue, ask the others for the answer and how they managed to get it (i.e., one student was attempting to answer a question related to cereals, and she found the answer by looking at cereal boxes; another student used a CD-ROM as a tool; another knew the answer because he had just finished reading a book and had encountered the exact word that the puzzle was asking for)
- by discussing the "how," students will acquire strategies that can be used in other activities
- this proves to be an effective strategy because the students will often suggest strategies that the teacher may not have considered

Second:

- make an overhead transparency
- have a student read a clue, offer a solution, and, if it's correct, spell it
- print the answer with a washable overhead marker
- continue this process until the activity is corrected

Follow Up

- challenge some students to make an activity
- once they have experienced two or three Pair of Diamond activities, and once they have an understanding of how the activity is set up, provide them with a diamond template and encourage them to develop good clues for their answers
- once the activity has been made and conferenced, have them prepare a good copy that can be photocopied and distributed to the class
- very motivational—students love to see their names in print

Name: ____________________ Date: ____________

Pair of Diamonds Puzzle: *Holiday Greetings*

Directions: Read and answer each of the clues carefully. When finished, read down the left side of each diamond to reveal a hidden message. Copy the message onto the lines at the bottom of the page.

1
2
3
4
5
6
7
8
9
10
11
12
13
14
15
16
17

LEFT DIAMOND

1. Roman numeral for 1000
2. A comparative ending
3. Not cooked; in natural state
4. Not cooked much; not usually seen
5. Contraction for you are
6. Long form for can't
7. Synonym for vacation
8. Person belonging to the same family
9. Meaning much; having social position
10. A male horse
11. Frighten very much; fill with fear
12. Very small; an extremely small person
13. A person who acts on stage and TV
14. Homonym for sore
15. A playing card having the "one" spot
16. Antonym for yes
17. Roman numeral for 500

RIGHT DIAMOND

1. Symbol for hour or hours
2. Opposite of B.C.
3. A chum; playmate; comrade
4. Homonym for pair
5. A young man; young people
6. Ten times nine
7. Clear; plain; easy to understand
8. Marriage ceremonies
9. The day before today
10. A person who makes or runs engines
11. A person born or living in Africa
12. Say "no" to; reject
13. Help to learn; give lessons in
14. A solemn promise
15. Advertisements
16. Sixth tone of the musical scale
17. Roman numeral for 50

Name: ______________________________ Date: ________________

Pair of Diamonds Puzzle: *Lunch Specials*

Directions: Read and answer each of the clues carefully. When finished, read down the left side of each diamond to reveal a hidden message. Copy the message onto the lines at the bottom of the page.

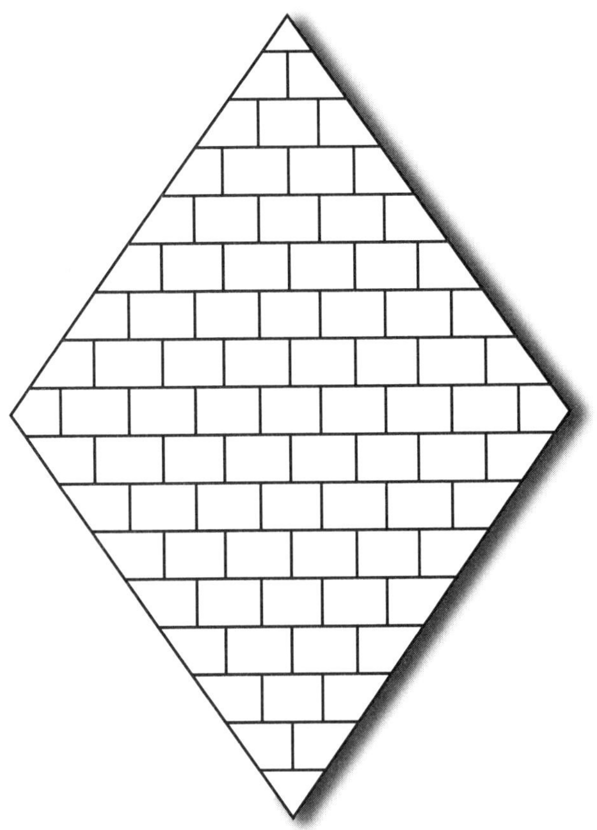

1
2
3
4
5
6
7
8
9
10
11
12
13
14
15
16
17

LEFT DIAMOND

1. Abbreviation for page
2. Contraction for I would
3. A place where animals are kept
4. Nought; the figure "0"
5. Behind; later; following
6. Frightened; feeling fear
7. Recently or only just born
8. A heavy rainfall
9. Greenhouses
10. A short amusing opera
11. Make tight; become tight
12. Male ducks
13. Leaves out
14. Smiles broadly
15. Antonym for night
16. Abbreviation for alternating current
17. 25th letter of the alphabet

RIGHT DIAMOND

1. Symbol for second or seconds
2. Abbreviation for time from midnight to noon
3. Past tense of run
4. The direction of the sunrise
5. The lowest female voices
6. Full of thorns
7. To build again
8. Eight more than ten
9. Great surprise; sudden wonder
10. Long form for they've
11. Buddies; pals; chums
12. The East; the countries in Asia
13. Prepared; willing; likely
14. Spouse of a queen
15. Sick, not well
16. Abbreviation for drive
17. Abbreviation for south or southern

_ _ _ _ _ _   _ _ _ _   _ _ _ _   _ _ _ _   _ _ _ _ _

_ _ _ _   _   _ _ _ _ _ _ _ _   _ _ _ _   _ _ _ _ _.

Name: ______________________________ Date: ________________

Pair of Diamonds Puzzle: *Best Friends*

Directions: Read and answer each of the clues carefully. When finished, read down the left side of each diamond to reveal a hidden message. Copy the message onto the lines at the bottom of the page.

1
2
3
4
5
6
7
8
9
10
11
12
13
14
15
16
17

LEFT DIAMOND

1. Abbreviation for east or eastern
2. Preposition meaning in; on; by or near
3. Cut roughly; tear apart
4. A breathing organ found in the chest
5. Antonym for old
6. A pointed, hanging stick of ice
7. Produced by nature; like nature
8. The fifth day of the week
9. Ground beef
10. Raises; lifts up
11. A triangle with three unequal sides
12. Cold; unpleasantly cool
13. Homonym for herd
14. One time; at some time in the past
15. Abbreviation for October
16. A suffix meaning "in a way or manner"
17. 25th letter of the alphabet

RIGHT DIAMOND

1. Fifth letter of the alphabet
2. To the same degree; equally
3. Be freed from; make free
4. Homonym for fore
5. An instrument used for shaving
6. A baby; a very young child
7. Make larger; grow larger
8. A short form of a proper name
9. Hard to do or understand
10. In the second place
11. A story in a newspaper or magazine
12. Go back; come back
13. Be happy with; take pleasure in
14. Change from solid to liquid
15. You're = you ______
16. The first or last tone of the musical scale
17. The first letter of the direction of the sunrise

___ ___ ___ ___ ___ ___   ___ ___   ___ ___ ___   ___ ___ ___ ___ ___ ___   ___ ___ ___ ___

___ ___ ___ ___ ___ ___ ___ ___   ___ ___ ___   ___ ___ ___ ___.

Name: ______________________________ Date: ____________________

Pair of Diamonds Puzzle: *Witches and Goblins*

Directions: Read and answer each of the clues carefully. When finished, read down the left side of each diamond to reveal a hidden message. Copy the message onto the lines at the bottom of the page.

1
2
3
4
5
6
7
8
9
10
11
12
13
14
15
16
17

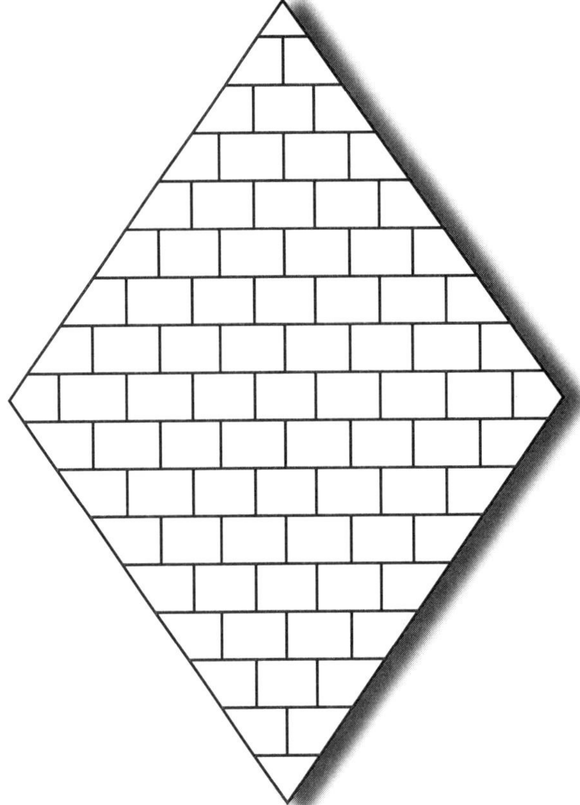

LEFT DIAMOND

1. One-letter word for *one* or *each*
2. Sixth tone of the musical scale
3. A boy; a young man
4. The price paid
5. A muscular organ that pumps blood
6. Turn upside down; reverse in direction
7. A small red/orange beetle with black spots
8. A young duck
9. An oval piece of ground used for racing
10. Opposite of westward
11. Tell a story
12. A person who makes or repairs clothes
13. Large farm for raising cattle, sheep, and horses
14. A plan or picture in the mind
15. Synonym for taxi
16. Symbol for kilogram or kilograms
17. Zero

RIGHT DIAMOND

1. The letter that appears twice in rare
2. Seventh tone of the musical scale
3. A torn piece of waste cloth
4. A sounding again; be repeated in sound
5. The nut of an oak tree
6. Special natural ability
7. A sea animal with eight arms
8. A poison contained in tobacco
9. A mischievous elf; goblin
10. A huge snake; a kind of boa
11. A one-piece garment worn by dancers
12. Young animals born at the same time
13. A play that is mostly sung
14. Wild animal resembling a large dog
15. Antonym for begin
16. A suffix meaning "past tense"
17. Abbreviation for north or northern

___ ___ ___   ___ ___ ___ ___ ___ ___ ___ ___   ___ ___ ___ ___ ___   ___ ___

___ ___ ___ ___ ___   ___ ___   ___ ___ ___ ___ ___ ___ ___ ___ ___.

Name: ______________________ Date: ______________

Pair of Diamonds Puzzle: *March Madness*

Directions: Read and answer each of the clues carefully. When finished, read down the left side of each diamond to reveal a hidden message. Copy the message onto the lines at the bottom of the page.

LEFT DIAMOND

1. Abbreviation for ton or tons
2. An exclamation of surprise or joy
3. A female sheep
4. A list of food served at a restaurant
5. The joint that connects the foot with the leg
6. Done, made, or happening not long ago
7. Black insect related to a grasshopper
8. Spears with ropes attached, used for hunting whales
9. Pirate; a robber on the sea
10. Plant again with trees
11. Hug; hold in the arms
12. Antonym for question
13. Mix bread by pressing and stretching
14. Appliance used to smooth wrinkles from clothing
15. Break the law of God
16. Abbreviation for advertisement
17. Exactly or perfectly; to a ______

RIGHT DIAMOND

1. Homonym for eye
2. Abbreviation for Doctor of Medicine
3. A large flightless Australian bird
4. Work hard; labor
5. Bulb-like plant with strong smell and taste
6. Recycle, ______, reuse
7. No longer existing
8. A person who owns buildings and rents them out
9. Gave up completely; deserted
10. A short form for "Christmas time"
11. Do; carry out; reach a goal
12. Slang for a very stupid person
13. Not clean; soiled by mud or dirt
14. A small horse
15. Move too slowly; fall behind
16. Opposite of p.m.
17. 25th letter of the alphabet

___ ___ ___   ___ ___ ___ ___ ___   ___ ___ ___ ___ ___   ___ ___   ___   ___ ___ ___ ___

___ ___   ___ ___ ___ ___ ___   ___ ___ ___   ___ ___ ___ ___.

Name: ______________________________ Date: ________________

Pair of Diamonds Puzzle: *Summer Fun*

Directions: Read and answer each of the clues carefully. When finished, read down the left side of each diamond to reveal a hidden message. Copy the message onto the lines at the bottom of the page.

1
2
3
4
5
6
7
8
9
10
11
12
13
14
15
16
17

LEFT DIAMOND

1. The second letter of the alphabet
2. Initials of Adam Anderson
3. Antonym for happy
4. A way out
5. Opposite of white
6. A disease causing difficulty in breathing
7. A sea creature having two big claws
8. Sucker; hard candy on a stick
9. A helper; an aide
10. The eleventh month
11. A qualified person who examines teeth
12. A very bad smell; stink
13. Atlantic or Pacific
14. Quiet; still; not stormy
15. Vehicle; automobile
16. Abbreviation for emergency room
17. Letter between q and s

RIGHT DIAMOND

1. The most used letter in asparagus
2. Abbreviation for road
3. Evening; the evening before a holiday
4. Gentle; kind; warm; not harsh
5. Contraction for you are
6. Great desert in the north of Africa
7. Not sound; not in good condition
8. To learn by heart
9. A drink made of milk and ice cream
10. A huge strong animal of Africa
11. Very quickly; swiftly
12. Make a loud, piercing cry
13. A heavy winter jacket with a hood
14. Long form for O.K.
15. A male sheep
16. Homonym for too or two
17. Symbol for second or seconds

Name: ____ Date: ____________________

Pair of Diamonds Puzzle: *Two Hundred Days of the Year*

Directions: Read and answer each of the clues carefully. When finished, read down the left side of each diamond to reveal a hidden message. Copy the message onto the lines at the bottom of the page.

1
2
3
4
5
6
7
8
9
10
11
12
13
14
15
16
17

LEFT DIAMOND

1. The most used letter in eighteen
2. Abbreviation for Victoria Cross
3. Abbreviation for et cetera
4. Homonym for reed
5. A possessive form of you
6. Run quickly; scamper
7. Grassy land where cattle and sheep feed
8. Completely; totally
9. A sour, dark red sauce eaten with turkey
10. Not mature; not fully grown
11. Something made a long time ago
12. How long something is
13. Cotton cloth used to make jeans
14. A region; a level surface or space
15. A kind of sweet potato
16. Initials for compact disc
17. Motion picture rating (Restricted)

RIGHT DIAMOND

1. Abbreviation for east or eastern
2. An advertisement
3. Light yellowish-brown
4. Bad; something bad; wrong
5. Equipment used by underwater swimmers
6. Next after first
7. Contraction for could not
8. Polygons with six sides
9. A large group of musicians
10. Heat too much
11. Suitcases; bags; baggage
12. Teeter-totter
13. A field of rice
14. Appliance used to smooth wrinkles from clothing
15. The color of blood
16. Contraction for I would
17. Twentieth letter of the alphabet

_ _ _ _ _   _ _ _ _ _ _ _ _   _ _ _

_ _ _ _ _ _ _   _ _ _ _ _ _   _ _ _ _ _ _.

Name: ______________________________ Date: ________________

Pair of Diamonds Puzzle: *Cupid's Special Day*

Directions: Read and answer each of the clues carefully. When finished, read down the left side of each diamond to reveal a hidden message. Copy the message onto the lines at the bottom of the page.

1
2
3
4
5
6
7
8
9
10
11
12
13
14
15
16
17

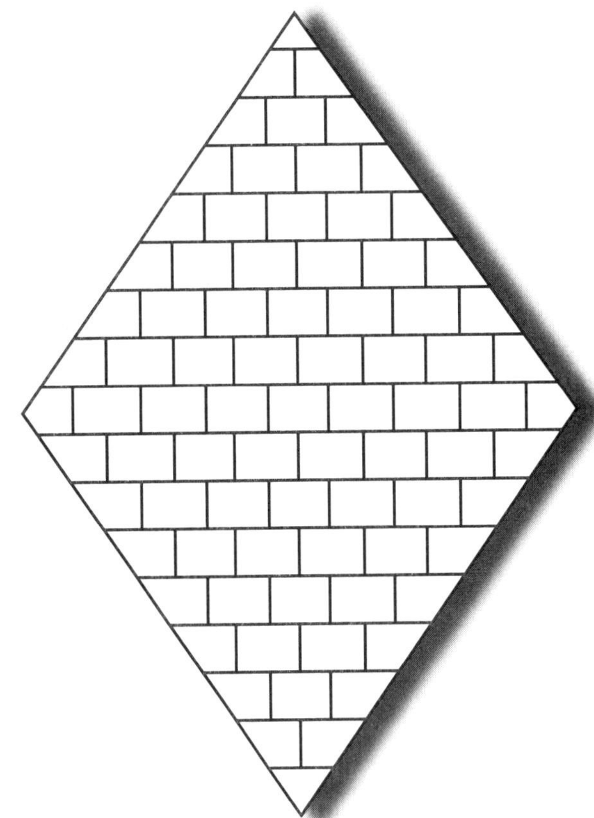

LEFT DIAMOND

1. (Song title) The letter that precedes "Canada"
2. Opposite of yes
3. Force; energy; vigor
4. Small insects that live in tunnels
5. Awkwardly long and thin
6. A hard try; attempt
7. Not anything; a thing of no value
8. Gifted; having natural ability
9. Meeting between parent and teacher
10. Eleventh month of the year
11. Raise; lift up
12. The highest point; the top
13. The distance from top to bottom
14. A word said at the end of a prayer
15. A coniferous tree pronounced like "you"
16. Abbreviation for week
17. Fifth letter of the alphabet

RIGHT DIAMOND

1. The first two letters of aardvark
2. Sixth tone of the musical scale
3. Allow; permit
4. Past tense of give
5. An Inuit house or hut
6. Cloth with thick, soft pile
7. An imaginary circle around the middle of the earth
8. A person who uses magic
9. Large ape with very long arms
10. *Time*, *People*, or *National Geographic*
11. At last; at the end
12. Not a solid or a gas
13. A fertile spot in the desert
14. Contraction for will not
15. Female sheep
16. Sun god of ancient Egypt
17. Suffix that makes a noun plural

Name: ______________________________________ Date: ____________________

Combination Puzzle: *Analogous Relationships #1*

Directions: The grid below consists of 24 squares with each square containing three letters. The three letters make up the first portion of a word or the last portion. Your task is to match up the portions and create 12 six-letter words. As you find the words, write your answers in any of the spaces provided in the second grid. One has already been done for you as an example.

~~MIN~~	MER	HER	SEV	BLA	OUT
ERT	RED	SEN	POL	RID	GLE
ITE	HOR	JUN	~~UTE~~	HAM	LES
ERE	DEV	DLE	EXP	GAT	SAD

minute			

Directions: Use the above answers to complete the analogous relationships below. Think how the capitalized words belong together. From the above answers, find a word that is related to the italicized word in the same way.

1. PLUMP is to STOUT as *tiny* is to ___*minute*___.
2. EXPECTED is to STARTLING as *mild* is to ____________________.
3. CONFIDENT is to CERTAIN as *adept* is to ____________________.
4. MELLOW is to SOFTEN as *dwindle* is to ____________________.
5. BUILD is to RAZE as *strew* is to ____________________.
6. CAMEL is to DESERT as *elephant* is to ____________________.
7. CRAZY is to SANE as *impudent* is to ____________________.
8. CANNIBAL is to SAVAGE as *nun* is to ____________________.
9. NOOSE is to LASSO as *stirrup* is to ____________________.
10. HARD is to SEVERE as *nasty* is to ____________________.
11. BELL is to CLANGED as *bugle* is to ____________________.
12. RIDGE is to FILE as *claw* is to ____________________.

Name: ______________________ Date: ______________

Combination Puzzle: *Analogous Relationships #2*

Directions: The grid below consists of 24 squares with each square containing three letters. The three letters make up the first portion of a word or the last portion. Your task is to match up the portions and create 12 six-letter words. As you find the words, write your answers in any of the spaces provided in the second grid. One has already been done for you as an example.

GEN	DEN	GUI	~~CIR~~	QUI	ACT
SIM	LID	COL	EXT	AFF	BLE
END	VER	PEB	IUS	PLE	EYE
IRM	~~CUS~~	IMP	SUD	TAR	UMN

circus			

Directions: Use the above answers to complete the analogous relationships below. Think how the capitalized words belong together. From the above answers, find a word that is related to the italicized word in the same way.

1. BRONCO is to STABLE as *tiger* is to <u>circus</u>.
2. DIFFICULT is to COMPLEX as *easy* is to ______________.
3. DAM is to BARRIER as *collision* is to ______________.
4. SEAM is to STITCH as *newspaper* is to ______________.
5. WATER is to HYDRANT as *arrow* is to ______________.
6. DISEASE is to PLAGUE as *expert* is to ______________.
7. DIMINISH is to INCREASE as *contradict* is to ______________.
8. DEPRESS is to PIANO as *strum* is to ______________.
9. SWALLOW is to THROAT as *blink* is to ______________.
10. FROWN is to SCOWL as *lengthen* is to ______________.
11. BOUGH is to TWIG as *boulder* is to ______________.
12. EXTINGUISH is to QUENCH as *abrupt* is to ______________.

Name: ______________________________ Date: ______________

Combination Puzzle: *Analogous Relationships #3*

Directions: The grid below consists of 24 squares with each square containing three letters. The three letters make up the first portion of a word or the last portion. Your task is to match up the portions and create 12 six-letter words. As you find the words, write your answers in any of the spaces provided in the second grid. One has already been done for you as an example.

~~ARD~~	MAS	ARD	ENT	TWE	DLE
WSE	TER	NTY	FAL	EST	WIZ
ADV	FOR	CAM	ICE	QUA	ERA
REC	RRY	HAN	DRO	~~REW~~	TER

reward			

Directions: Use the above answers to complete the analogous relationships below. Think how the capitalized words belong together. From the above answers, find a word that is related to the italicized word in the same way.

1. DEMERIT is to PENALTY as *bonus* is to *reward*.
2. DIVIDE is to SPLIT as *counsel* is to ____________________.
3. CENTURY is to HUNDRED as *score* is to ____________________.
4. WIDOW is to WIDOWER as *witch* is to ____________________.
5. CADET is to OFFICER as *apprentice* is to ____________________.
6. BANK is to VAULT as *skillet* is to ____________________.
7. OLD is to ANCIENT as *current* is to ____________________.
8. ARGUMENT is to DISPUTE as *prey* is to ____________________.
9. TACK is to SPIKE as *grove* is to ____________________.
10. CHIP is to SPLINTER as *sleep* is to ____________________.
11. CURRENT is to STREAM as *film* is to ____________________.
12. HIDE is to CONCEAL as *hesitate* is to ____________________.

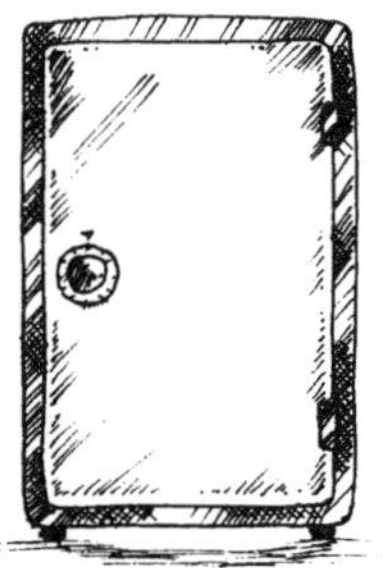

Name: ______________________________ Date: ______________

Combination Puzzle: *Analogous Relationships #4*

Directions: The grid below consists of 24 squares with each square containing three letters. The three letters make up the first portion of a word or the last portion. Your task is to match up the portions and create 12 six-letter words. As you find the words, write your answers in any of the spaces provided in the second grid. One has already been done for you as an example.

KED	ORT	MSY	DED	BID	DIV
DER	STA	~~WEI~~	WIC	LAD	LIQ
ACH	UID	RET	FFS	BLE	STU
BEA	DER	IDE	BLE	CLU	~~GHT~~

weight			

Directions: Use the above answers to complete the analogous relationships below. Think how the capitalized words belong together. From the above answers, find a word that is related to the italicized word in the same way.

1. DEGREE is to TEMPERATURE as *pound* is to *weight*.
2. COURT is to WITNESS as *auction* is to ______________.
3. GLANCE is to STARE as *naughty* is to ______________.
4. BEEF is to SOLID as *juice* is to ______________.
5. WITHDRAW is to DEPOSIT as *dye* is to ______________.
6. LABOR is to TOIL as *separate* is to ______________.
7. ROOST is to COOP as *stall* is to ______________.
8. REPAIRED is to DARNED as *trimmed* is to ______________.
9. INNER is to INTERNAL as *awkward* is to ______________.
10. ATTACK is to RAID as *reply* is to ______________.
11. RECLINE is to BED as *climb* is to ______________.
12. DOZES is to DROWSES as *crams* is to ______________.

Name: ________________________________ Date: ________________

Combination Puzzle: *Analogous Relationships #5*

Directions: The grid below consists of 24 squares with each square containing three letters. The three letters make up the first portion of a word or the last portion. Your task is to match up the portions and create 12 six-letter words. As you find the words, write your answers in any of the spaces provided in the second grid. One has already been done for you as an example.

ART	REL	TER	BAT	CAN	KEN
ORB	YON	TEN	HOR	TER	~~REM~~
TLE	NEL	THA	ABS	BAR	WED
ROR	~~OTE~~	LET	IST	FIL	FAS

remote			

Directions: Use the above answers to complete the analogous relationships below. Think how the capitalized words belong together. From the above answers, find a word that is related to the italicized word in the same way.

1. NEAR is to CLOSE as *distant* is to ___*remote*___.
2. OPPONENT is to GAME as *foe* is to ______________.
3. TWIG is to BRANCH as *keg* is to ______________.
4. BORROWED is to LENT as *froze* is to ______________.
5. BENCH is to MACHINIST as *easel* is to ______________.
6. HOMELY is to UGLY as *dismay* is to ______________.
7. WAVE is to BILLOW as *gully* is to ______________.
8. BRIDLE is to BIT as *alphabet* is to ______________.
9. SHRED is to STRIP as *strain* is to ______________.
10. ARTIST is to STUDIO as *dog* is to ______________.
11. COUGH is to EXPEL as *clasp* is to ______________.
12. SPEEDOMETER is to INDICATE as *towel* is to ______________.

Name: ____________________ Date: ____________

Combination Puzzle: *Analogous Relationships #6*

Directions: The grid below consists of 24 squares with each square containing three letters. The three letters make up the first portion of a word or the last portion. Your task is to match up the portions and create 12 six-letter words. As you find the words, write your answers in any of the spaces provided in the second grid. One has already been done for you as an example.

CEM	GER	AYS	IOS	QUI	DEL
ORE	~~ADE~~	SIN	ENT	MEL	SIG
NAL	BLE	HAM	IGN	FIN	STA
VER	RAD	TED	~~DEC~~	GLE	MER

decade			

Directions: Use the above answers to complete the analogous relationships below. Think how the capitalized words belong together. From the above answers, find a word that is related to the italicized word in the same way.

1. TEN is to ONE as *century* is to ___decade___.
2. SKIP is to HOP as *tremble* is to ____________.
3. STARTS is to COMMENCES as *postpones* is to ____________.
4. CEREAL is to GRAIN as *concrete* is to ____________.
5. CUT is to KNIFE as *dent* is to ____________.
6. CHANNELS is to TELEVISIONS as *stations* is to ____________.
7. ZIPPER is to FASTENER as *beacon* is to ____________.
8. COUPLE is to PAIR as *one* is to ____________.
9. TRICKLED is to DRIPPED as *thawed* is to ____________.
10. FOOT is to TOE as *hand* is to ____________.
11. AGREE is to PROTEST as *consider* is to ____________.
12. LION is to DEN as *stallion* is to ____________.

Name: ______________________________ Date: ______________

Combination Puzzle: *Analogous Relationships #7*

Directions: The grid below consists of 24 squares with each square containing three letters. The three letters make up the first portion of a word or the last portion. Your task is to match up the portions and create 12 six-letter words. As you find the words, write your answers in any of the spaces provided in the second grid. One has already been done for you as an example.

ISL	MER	IGN	STR	DEF	SEN
NET	GAT	~~COS~~	SIM	JUD	PEP
IES	GED	IOR	AND	DES	RUB
ING	END	PER	~~TLY~~	GAR	HER

costly			

Directions: Use the above answers to complete the analogous relationships below. Think how the capitalized words belong together. From the above answers, find a word that is related to the italicized word in the same way.

1. SOGGY is to MOIST as *expensive* is to *costly*.
2. YELLOW is to AMBER as *red* is to ______________.
3. YOUNGER is to OLDER as *junior* is to ______________.
4. LEAP is to VAULT as *protect* is to ______________.
5. GREEN is to EMERALDS as *red* is to ______________.
6. THREAD is to YARN as *cord* is to ______________.
7. STREAM is to RIVER as *isle* is to ______________.
8. BUILD is to DESTROY as *scatter* is to ______________.
9. PORCH is to STOOP as *pattern* is to ______________.
10. STAGE is to ACTED as *court* is to ______________.
11. ORGAN is to HEART as *spice* is to ______________.
12. TORNADO is to GUST as *boil* is to ______________.

Name: ______________________________ Date: ________________

Combination Puzzle: *Analogous Relationships #8*

Directions: The grid below consists of 24 squares with each square containing three letters. The three letters make up the first portion of a word or the last portion. Your task is to match up the portions and create 12 six-letter words. As you find the words, write your answers in any of the spaces provided in the second grid. One has already been done for you as an example.

ING	GLE	ENT	MAN	DAR	AVE
UAL	FOL	DON	ADM	MES	~~GAL~~
SIN	~~LOP~~	FLA	DER	RAI	TAR
NUE	SIL	GUI	AMS	KEY	IRE

gallop			

Directions: Use the above answers to complete the analogous relationships below. Think how the capitalized words belong together. From the above answers, find a word that is related to the italicized word in the same way.

1. WHEEL is to ROTATE as *horse* is to ___*gallop*___.
2. ADULT is to YOUTH as *automatic* is to ________________.
3. SHY is to BASHFUL as *glitters* is to ________________.
4. RIVER is to BROOK as *road* is to ________________.
5. NEIGH is to HORSE as *bray* is to ________________.
6. BLIZZARD is to SNOW as *bold* is to ________________.
7. BOY is to GIRL as *scorn* is to ________________.
8. PLUM is to PRUNE as *grape* is to ________________.
9. LACES is to SHOE as *strings* is to ________________.
10. PALS is to FRIENDS as *sparks* is to ________________.
11. SCREEN is to TELEVISION as *tab* is to ________________.
12. SHUT is to SLAM as *quiet* is to ________________.

Name: ______________________________ Date: ______________

Clues Galore: *Build Your Vocabulary #1*

Directions: Read each clue and think of an answer. The number in parentheses in front of the clue tells you how many letters are in the answer. Write your answer on the spaces to the right of the clue. Fill in the numbered boxes with the letter from each of the clues provided and arrive at a nine-letter answer.

1	2	3	4	5	6	7	8	9
	U	*R*	*F*					

(3) soft, hairy coat of certain animals — *F* *U* *R* (4 2 3)

(4) to make a loud, deep sound or noise — __ __ __ __ (3 6 7 8)

(4) small swellings on a plant — __ __ __ __ (5 2 9 1)

(5) a person who tricks or cheats — __ __ __ __ __ (4 3 7 2 9)

B

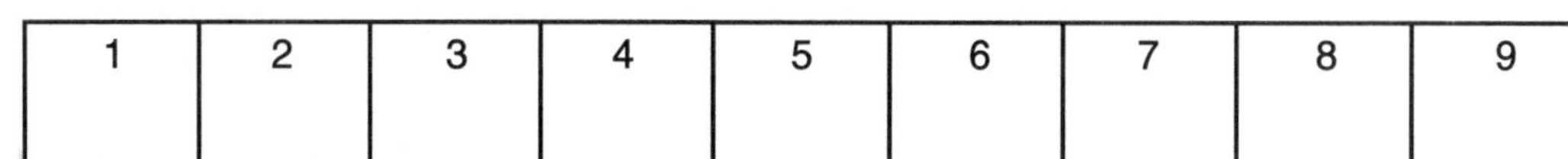

(5) a kind of whistle with a loud, shrill sound — __ __ __ __ __ (3 4 1 6 7)

(4) eat a special food or drink (to lose or gain weight) — __ __ __ __ (5 4 2 8)

(5) severe; strict; harsh — __ __ __ __ __ (9 8 2 1 7)

(5) eats dinner — __ __ __ __ __ (5 4 7 2 9)

C

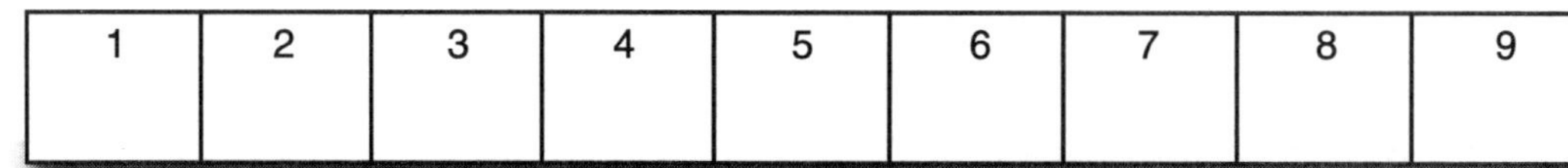

(4) crack open like skin; become rough like skin — __ __ __ __ (5 6 4 1)

(5) a map; a sheet of information arranged in pictures — __ __ __ __ __ (5 6 2 3 8)

(5) a large box used to pack furniture or fruit for shipping — __ __ __ __ __ (5 3 2 8 9)

(3) a small, roughly made house; a small cabin — __ __ __ (6 7 8)

Name: ______________________________ Date: ________________

Clues Galore: *Build Your Vocabulary #2*

Directions: Read each clue and think of an answer. The number in parentheses in front of the clue tells you how many letters are in the answer. Write your answer on the spaces to the right of the clue. Fill in the numbered boxes with the letter from each of the clues provided and arrive at a nine-letter answer.

1	2	3	4	5	6	7	8	9

(5) an old woman who is thin and withered ___ ___ ___ ___ ___ (4 3 2 8 9)

(4) a tube through which a liquid or gas passes ___ ___ ___ ___ (6 7 1 9)

(6) to come down with a rush and seize something ___ ___ ___ ___ ___ ___ (6 2 5 8 4 9)

(4) full-grown and ready to be gathered and eaten ___ ___ ___ ___ (3 7 6 9)

B

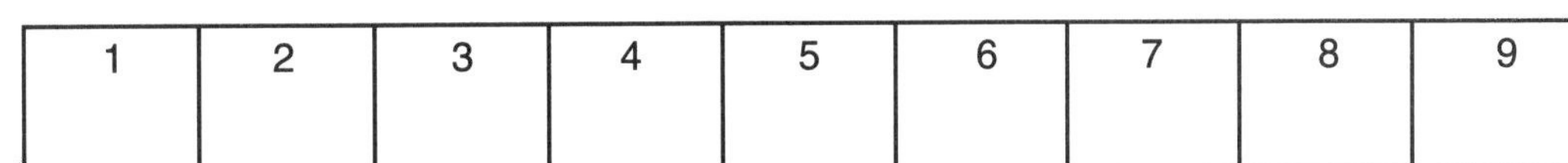

(4) put a value on; rank; estimate; consider ___ ___ ___ ___ (4 5 6 3)

(4) a strong, thick line or cord made of twisted fiber or wire ___ ___ ___ ___ (4 8 2 3)

(5) a connected line of railway cars pulled by an engine ___ ___ ___ ___ ___ (6 4 5 7 9)

(4) a single musical sound ___ ___ ___ ___ (9 1 6 3)

C

1	2	3	4	5	6	7	8	9

(5) in tennis, put the ball in play by hitting it ___ ___ ___ ___ ___ (8 9 5 6 4)

(5) something that can damage a computer ___ ___ ___ ___ ___ (6 7 5 2 1)

(4) a trick or stratagem ___ ___ ___ ___ (5 2 1 4)

(4) a structure built over the water where ships land ___ ___ ___ ___ (3 7 9 5)

Name: ______________________________ Date: ______________

Clues Galore: *Build Your Vocabulary #3*

Directions: Read each clue and think of an answer. The number in parentheses in front of the clue tells you how many letters are in the answer. Write your answer on the spaces to the right of the clue. Fill in the numbered boxes with the letter from each of the clues provided and arrive at a nine-letter answer.

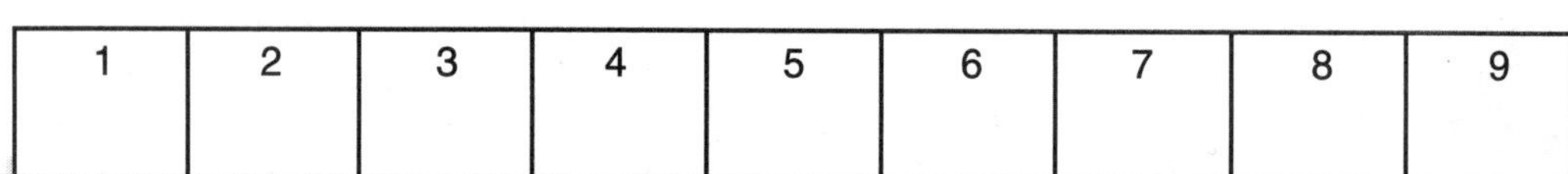

(4) run like water; glide; move easily ___ ___ ___ ___
4 5 6 7

(5) the past tense of swear ___ ___ ___ ___ ___
1 7 6 9 8

(3) playfulness; merry play; amusement ___ ___ ___
4 2 3

(4) melt or melt together by the action of heat ___ ___ ___ ___
4 2 1 8

B

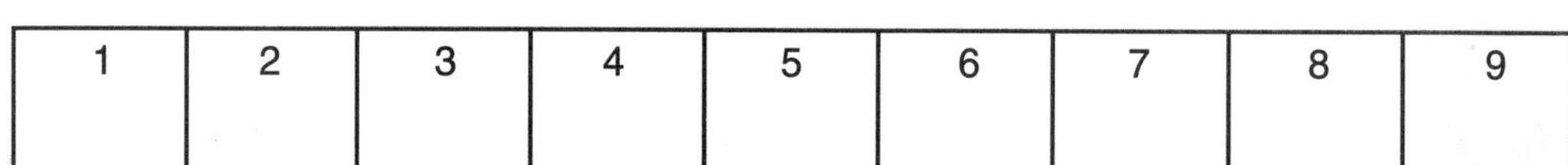

(3) an edge or border around anything ___ ___ ___
9 4 5

(5) opposite of composite number ___ ___ ___ ___ ___
1 3 4 5 8

(4) a homonym for team ___ ___ ___ ___
7 6 2 5

(4) come face to face with someone when walking ___ ___ ___ ___
5 2 6 7

C

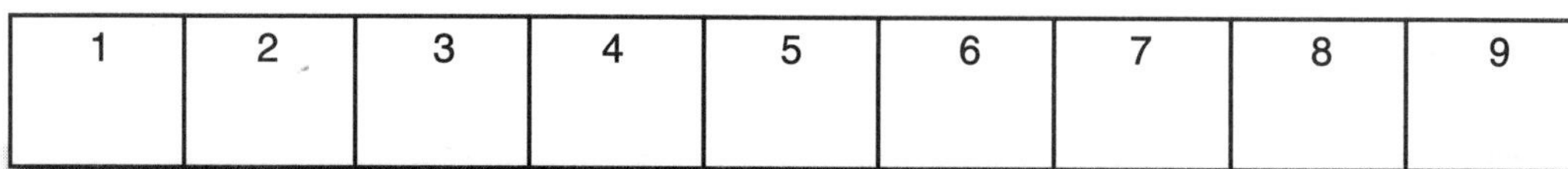

(5) seize; hold fast by closing fingers around ___ ___ ___ ___ ___
7 9 2 3 1

(4) that which determines hair color and skin color ___ ___ ___ ___
7 5 6 8

(3) droop; sink; sink under weight or pressure ___ ___ ___
4 2 7

(4) a state of violent anger ___ ___ ___ ___
9 2 7 5

Name: ______________________________ Date: ________________

Clues Galore: *Build Your Vocabulary #4*

Directions: Read each clue and think of an answer. The number in parentheses in front of the clue tells you how many letters are in the answer. Write your answer on the spaces to the right of the clue. Fill in the numbered boxes with the letter from each of the clues provided and arrive at a nine-letter answer.

A

1	2	3	4	5	6	7	8	9

Clue	Answer spaces
(4) antonym of female	__ __ __ __ (4 3 6 7)
(4) a dirty or untidy condition	__ __ __ __ (4 5 8 1)
(3) a girl or female already referred to	__ __ __ (9 2 5)
(4) close with a bang	__ __ __ __ (8 6 3 4)

B

1	2	3	4	5	6	7	8	9

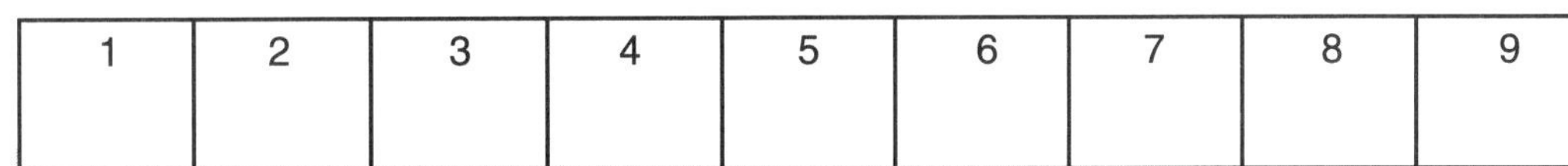

Clue	Answer spaces
(5) past tense of burn	__ __ __ __ __ (4 5 3 8 9)
(4) a long pipe of metal, glass, or rubber	__ __ __ __ (1 2 4 7)
(4) attract; tempt; attract with a bait	__ __ __ __ (6 5 3 7)
(4) not false	__ __ __ __ (1 3 5 7)

C

1	2	3	4	5	6	7	8	9

Clue	Answer spaces
(3) opposite of old	__ __ __ (8 3 4)
(4) liquid measurement equal to half a quart	__ __ __ __ (5 2 8 9)
(4) past tense of weave	__ __ __ __ (4 6 1 3)
(4) any of several evergreen trees	__ __ __ __ (5 7 8 3)

Name: ______________________________ Date: ____________________

Clues Galore: *Build Your Vocabulary #5*

Directions: Read each clue and think of an answer. The number in parentheses in front of the clue tells you how many letters are in the answer. Write your answer on the spaces to the right of the clue. Fill in the numbered boxes with the letter from each of the clues provided and arrive at a nine-letter answer.

1	2	3	4	5	6	7	8	9

(3) opposite of no ___ ___ ___ (9 5 3)

(5) buy and sell; the exchange of goods; commerce ___ ___ ___ ___ ___ (4 6 8 7 2)

(5) a substance that causes dough to rise ___ ___ ___ ___ ___ (1 2 8 3 4)

(3) the color of blood ___ ___ ___ (6 5 7)

B

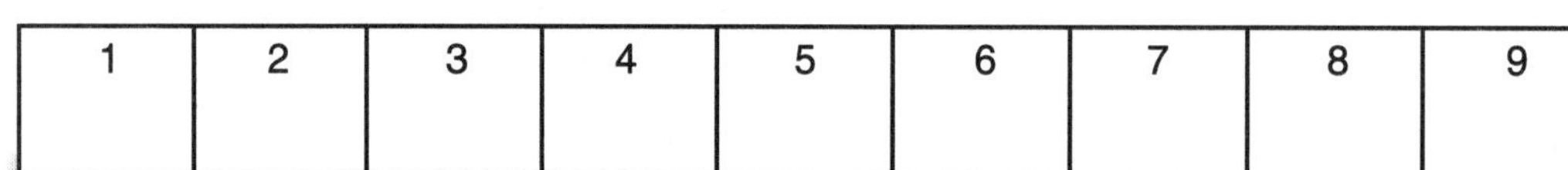

1	2	3	4	5	6	7	8	9

(4) the den of a wild animal ___ ___ ___ ___ (6 7 8 3)

(4) not imagined; actual; true ___ ___ ___ ___ (3 5 7 6)

(4) suffering in body or mind; cause to suffer ___ ___ ___ ___ (1 7 8 9)

(4) plants grown and gathered for use as food ___ ___ ___ ___ (4 3 2 1)

C

1	2	3	4	5	6	7	8	9

(4) expectation; anticipation ___ ___ ___ ___ (1 7 5 2)

(4) going a long way down from the top ___ ___ ___ ___ (4 9 2 5)

(4) the top part of the human ___ ___ ___ ___ (6 9 3 4)

(3) a writing instrument that supplies a flow of ink ___ ___ ___ (5 2 8)

Name: ______________________________ Date: ________________

Clues Galore: *Build Your Vocabulary #6*

Directions: Read each clue and think of an answer. The number in parentheses in front of the clue tells you how many letters are in the answer. Write your answer on the spaces to the right of the clue. Fill in the numbered boxes with the letter from each of the clues provided and arrive at a nine-letter answer.

1	2	3	4	5	6	7	8	9

(4) opposite of more ___ ___ ___ ___ (8 5 4 3)

(4) genuine; actual; not imagined ___ ___ ___ ___ (6 9 2 8)

(5) shut; come or bring to an end ___ ___ ___ ___ ___ (1 8 7 3 9)

(5) a group of students taught together ___ ___ ___ ___ ___ (1 8 2 3 4)

B

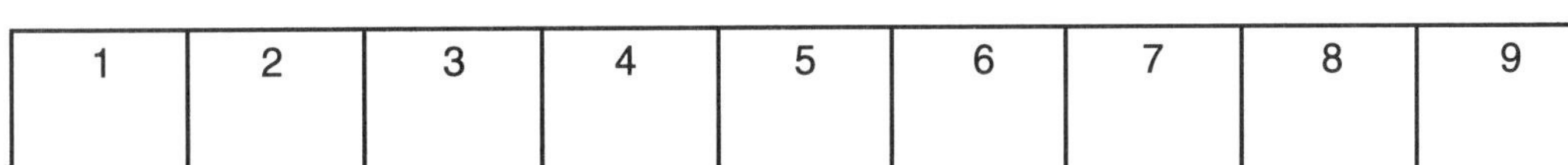

1	2	3	4	5	6	7	8	9

(4) to control; govern ___ ___ ___ ___ (8 7 4 1)

(4) part of the face that stands out above the mouth ___ ___ ___ ___ (2 5 6 9)

(4) antonym of win ___ ___ ___ ___ (4 5 6 1)

(5) a view; picture; a part of an act of a play ___ ___ ___ ___ ___ (6 3 9 2 1)

C

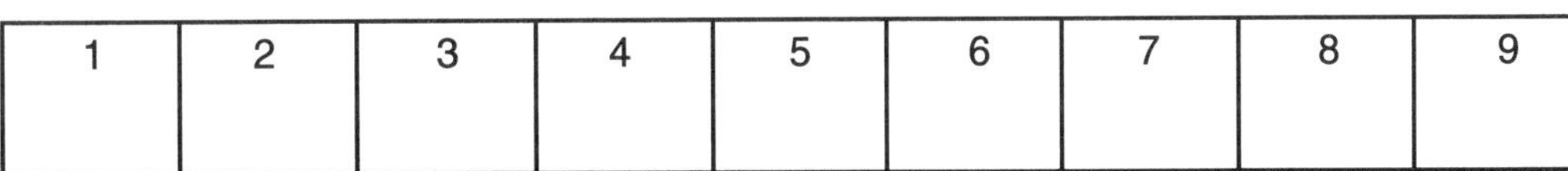

1	2	3	4	5	6	7	8	9

(4) the forehead ___ ___ ___ ___ (1 2 7 8)

(4) close; not far; not distant ___ ___ ___ ___ (9 3 4 2)

(5) a dark color like that of coffee or toast ___ ___ ___ ___ ___ (1 2 7 8 9)

(5) a male duck ___ ___ ___ ___ ___ (6 2 4 5 3)

Name: ______________________________ Date: ________________

Zig-Zag Topics: *Vocabulary Building #1*

Directions: Answer the clues correctly. Take the letters in order from each of the shaded areas and print them on the lines below. A message will appear.

O	*K*	*A*	*P*	*I*

1. having a sharp slope
2. words that name people, places, things, and ideas
3. juicy fruit belonging to the gourd family
4. a movable part that controls the flow of gas in a pipe
5. African mammal like a giraffe, smaller with a shorter neck
6. a bad smell
7. a sweet substance; a sweetener
8. antonym for full
9. an angle less than 90 degrees
10. homonym for stake
11. a person who shows people to their seats in a theater
12. run away to get married
13. a large pig-like animal with a flexible snout
14. first five letters of something seen in a dream
15. handles on doors and drawers
16. singular form of hollies
17. a lever worked by the foot
18. possibly or perhaps; it may be so
19. what remains after something has burned
20. to show the way; direct; lead
21. a brief stop; a rest
22. beat rapidly or strongly
23. land used for crops or pasture
24. a person born or living in Asia
25. a plant having daisy-like flowers with yellow centers
26. to clean with a broom or brush

___ ___ ___ ___ I ___ ___ ___ ___ ___ ___

___ ___ ___ ___ ___ ___ ___ ___ ___ ___ ___ ___ ___ ___ ___ ___.

Name: ______________________________ Date: ______________

Zig-Zag Topics: *Vocabulary Building #2*

Directions: Answer the clues correctly. Take the letters in order from each of the shaded areas and print them on the lines below. A message will appear.

1. respond or answer
2. one more than six
3. cloth worn around the shoulders
4. one of the divisions within a school
5. plural of cactus
6. past tense of sting
7. soaked; thoroughly wet
8. how wide something is
9. a smell; a smell left in passing
10. an Inuit canoe made of animal skins
11. contraction for has not
12. concentrate; adjust lens of a camera
13. a sweet, thick liquid
14. a seasoning used to flavor food
15. possessive form of you
16. not drunk
17. a white gem formed in an oyster
18. brand name for a duplicating/photocopying machine
19. backbone
20. take dishonestly
21. a large, dangerous fish
22. a very strong, flexible glass
23. tested; proved
24. burn a little (especially hair)
25. a view; picture; part of play
26. do very well; do better than others

___ ___ ___ ___ ___ ___ ___   ___ ___   ___   ___ ___ ___ ___ ___ ___

___ ___ ___ ___ ___ ___ ___ ___ ___ ___.

Name: ______________________________ Date: ________________

Zig-Zag Topics: *Vocabulary Building #3*

Directions: Answer the clues correctly. Take the letters in order from each of the shaded areas and print them on the lines below. A message will appear.

1. poetry with some lines ending in similar sounds
2. force back; drive back
3. salted and smoked meat from pigs
4. brightness; luster; shine
5. attics; the upper floors of warehouses
6. precedes second
7. play pranks; deceive; cheat
8. something of value; property
9. a grown-up person
10. not easily bent or moved
11. slightly wet; damp
12. spacious; large
13. a little bag for carrying money; handbag
14. a flat, narrow fold made by doubling material on itself
15. flower; blossom
16. acid-tasting, light yellow fruit
17. prepared; immediately available
18. a mistake; something done that is wrong
19. seat without back or arms
20. propose; suggest; present
21. comes after second
22. the most common language of India
23. cooked in hot oil
24. Saint Nicholas
25. French word for goodbye
26. very holy person

___ ___ ___ ___ ___ ___ ___ ___ ___ ___ ___ ___ ___ ___ ___ ___

___ ___ ___ ___ ___ ___ ___ ___ ___ ___ ___.

Name: ______________________________ Date: ______________

Zig-Zag Topics: *Vocabulary Building #4*

Directions: Answer the clues correctly. Take the letters in order from each of the shaded areas and print them on the lines below. A message will appear.

1. an appliance used for cooking
2. excellent; wonderful
3. a prank; trick; leap or jump about
4. a servant or hotel worker
5. person who makes bread, cakes, and pies
6. implements used to arrange hair
7. puts one's name on; writes one's name
8. a cloth with a smooth, glossy side
9. covered with mist
10. plural of tooth
11. a sticky sap from coniferous trees
12. speaking or spoken through the nose
13. a back tooth with a flat surface
14. opposite of nephew
15. suitable for a man
16. nemesis; foe
17. not clear; not distinct
18. homonym for rein and rain
19. joint that connects the foot with the leg
20. watchful; wide awake
21. notes with messages given on special days
22. more than one cactus
23. a liquid applied to a surface to add color
24. a heathen; one who worships more than one god
25. a sweet, thick liquid
26. singular form of monies

___ ___ ___ ___ ___ ___   ___ ___ ___ ___ ___   ___ ___ ___

___ ___ ___ ___ ___ ___ ___   ___ ___   ___ ___ ___.

Name: ______________________________ Date: ____________________

Zig-Zag Topics: *Scrambled Words #1*

Directions: Unscramble each of the words correctly. Take the letters in order from each of the shaded areas and print them on the lines below. A message will appear.

1. TEENA
2. LEXIE
3. NEREG
4. SENRT
5. NIPAC
6. DIMIT
7. ASONM
8. EHRAT
9. LOOGI
10. SPANE
11. PYIGG
12. RASEH
13. PACEL
14. IZAPZ
15. STYMI
16. ERFFO
17. TTSOA
18. GREAN
19. PAMTS
20. TOREH
21. ERRAC
22. CANRH
23. FERER
24. STOAR
25. UOPGR
26. BATEL

___ ___ ___ ___ ___ ___ ___ ___ ___   ___ ___   ___ ___ ___ ___ ___

___ ___ ___   ___ ___ ___   ___ ___ ___ ___ ___.

Name: ______________________________ Date: ____________________

Zig-Zag Topics: *Scrambled Words #2*

Directions: Unscramble each of the words correctly. Take the letters in order from each of the shaded areas and print them on the lines below. A message will appear.

1. G O A N Y
2. R O N A P
3. O C F R E
4. F O T E N
5. T U M S P
6. L I A R T
7. F H T O R
8. L R E A X
9. A W R N D
10. E N O P S
11. U E R N P
12. A D P E R
13. I G F U N
14. R O I L B
15. E J Y L L
16. M D E R A
17. Y A D B L
18. P A D R I
19. E L G A N
20. U S M I C
21. L O V E N
22. A M E D I
23. O M I T S
24. I V E L O
25. T O L I P
26. E A R N Y

___ ___ ___ ___ ___ ___ ___ ___ ___ ___ ___ ___ ___ ___

___ ___ ___ ___ ___ ___ ___ ___ ___ ___ ___ ___.

Name: ______________________________ Date: ________________

Last Letter-First Letter Puzzle: *Animals Galore*

Directions: Read each clue and think of an answer. The last letter of one word will always become the first letter of the next word. To decode the puzzle, write the shaded letters (in the order they appear in the puzzle) in the boxes below. This will reveal the name of a famous mascot.

1				2 N	A	R	W	H	A	3 L		

1. bird with a rusty-red breast
2. small arctic whale; male has a long tusk
3. an edible sea creature with two big claws
4. a male sheep
5. a very large animal of the deer family
6. an animal with floppy ears, tusks, and a trunk
7. resembles a frog but lives mostly on land
8. related to the horse but smaller with long ears
9. large, long-haired animal from Central Asia
10. Australian animal with great leaping ability
11. the largest of living birds
12. African animal that makes a cry that sounds like laughter
13. an African ant eater
14. Australian animal that lives in trees and eats eucalyptus leaves
15. a small burrowing animal with a very hard shell
16. a sea animal with eight tentacles
17. a bushy-tailed animal that usually lives in trees
18. a reptile with a long body, long tail, and movable eyelids
19. a doe and a buck are members of what family?

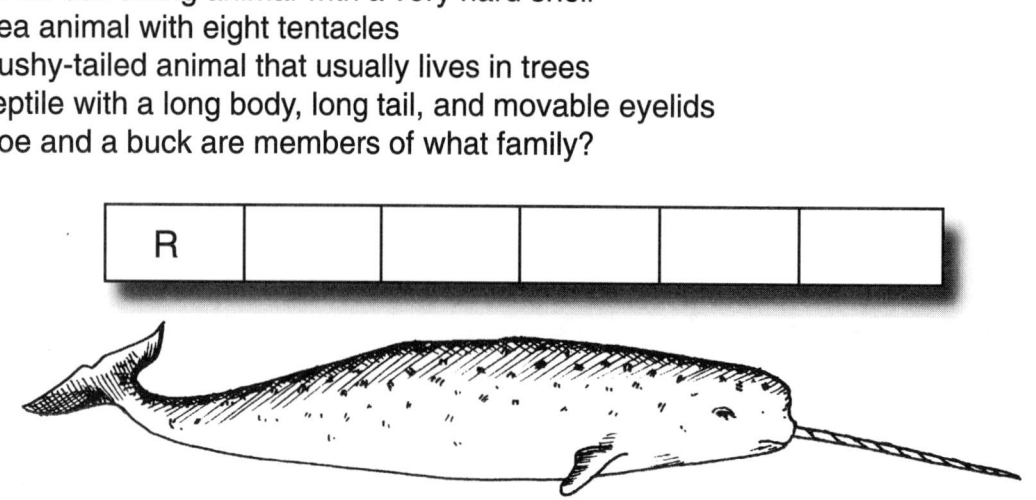

R					

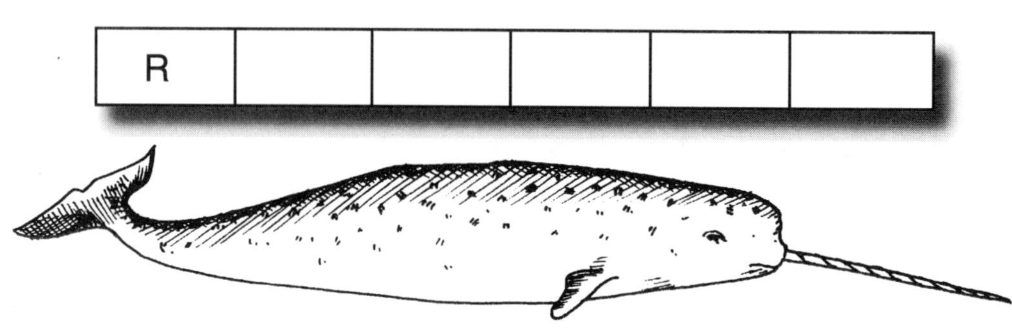

Name: ______________________ Date: ______________

Last Letter-First Letter Puzzle: *Law Enforcement*

Directions: Read each clue and think of an answer. The last letter of one word will always become the first letter of the next word. To decode the puzzle, write the shaded letters (in the order they appear in the puzzle) in the boxes below. This will reveal some bulletproof items that police officers use.

1. police officers whose job is investigating crimes
2. go about in a sneaking or prying way
3. shield from harm or danger
4. give evidence or proof before a judge
5. a child; a young person
6. a beginner, such as a new player on a team
7. unexpected events that call for immediate attention
8. not drunk
9. having no pity; showing no mercy
10. make a loud, sharp, piercing cry
11. a member of the Royal Canadian Mounted Police

12. skillful or wise because of experience; expert; practiced
13. destroy the peace, quiet, or rest of
14. marks or stains left by blood

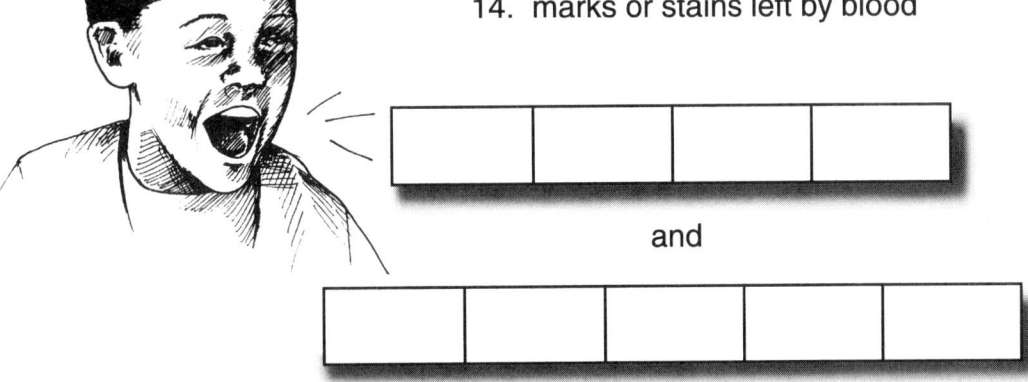

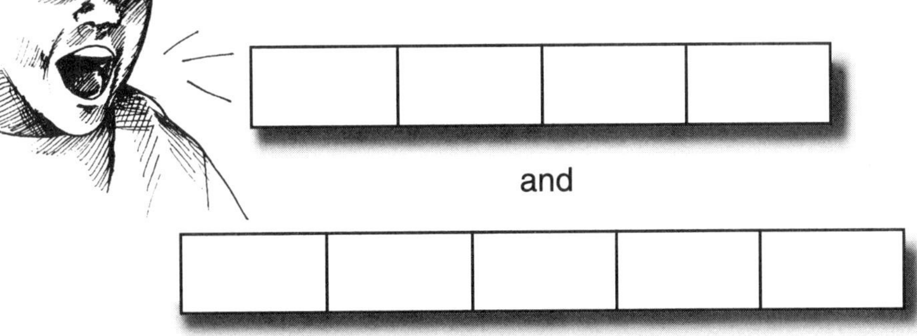

Name: ______________________________ Date: ________________

Last Letter-First Letter Puzzle: *Clothing and Accessories*

Directions: Read each clue and think of an answer. The last letter of one word will always become the first letter of the next word. To decode the puzzle, write the shaded letters (in the order they appear in the puzzle) in the boxes below. This will reveal the name of a tight-fitting jacket that holds the arms of a violent person close to his or her side.

1. a short coat
2. pants; slacks
3. a garment for the upper part of the body made of light material
4. a shaped, folded length of cloth worn under a collar
5. an ornament for the ear
6. a woman's dress; a loose outer garment
7. a string of jewels, gold, silver, beads, etc., worn around the neck
8. coverings put over the ears to keep them warm
9. a set of clothes to be worn together
10. a scarf wound around the head, worn by men in India and other countries
11. a loose garment worn in bed by boys and men
12. Some people have poor ______ in clothing.
13. spectacles; a pair of lenses worn in front of the eyes to help a person's vision
14. a shoe made of a sole and a strap or straps
15. a one-piece, close-fitting garment worn by dancers
16. an outer garment worn by women, girls, and babies
17. a piece of silk, wool, etc., worn about the neck, shoulders, or the head
18. one of the light, thin growths that cover a bird's skin

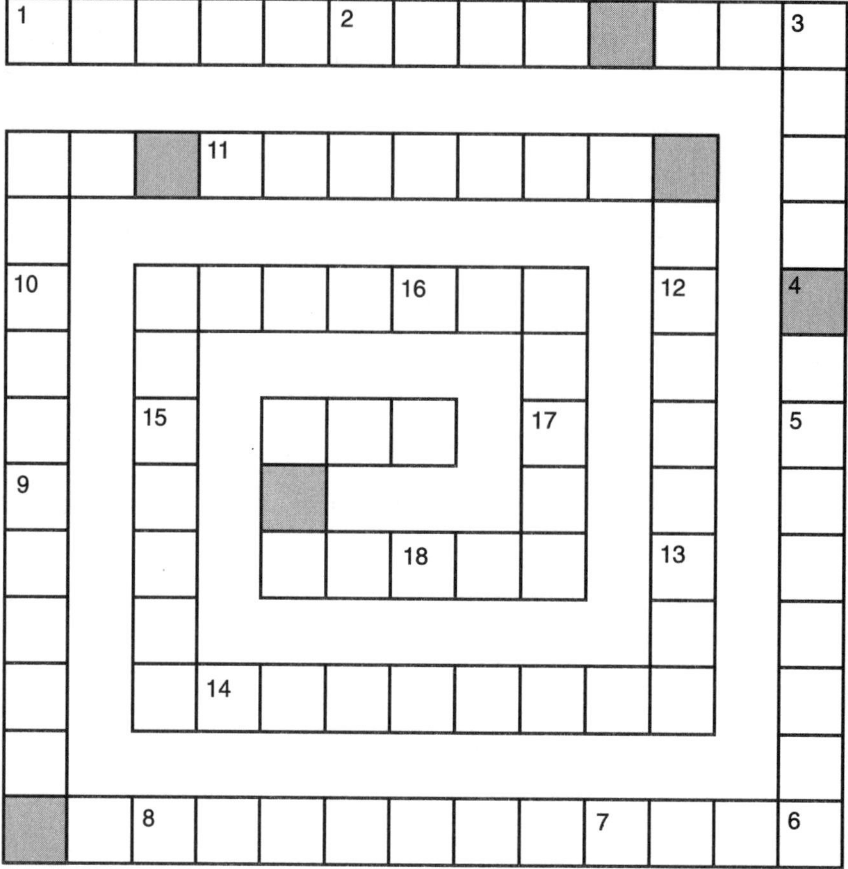

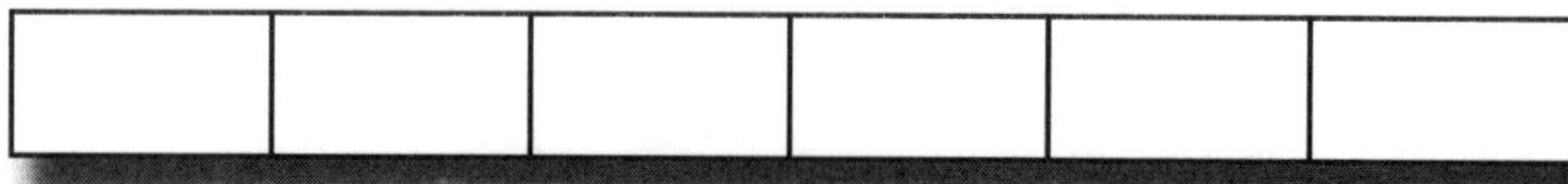

Name: ______________________________ Date: ________________

Last Letter-First Letter Puzzle: *Anyone Hungry?*

Directions: Read each clue and think of an answer. The last letter of one word will always become the first letter of the next word. To decode the puzzle, write the shaded letters (in the order they appear in the puzzle) in the boxes below. This will reveal the name of a favorite meat served to family and friends.

1. round, hard, starchy vegetables with brown skins
2. a thick slice of beef, usually broiled or barbecued
3. a sauce made from onions, tomatoes, salt, sugar, and spices
4. a long, tapered, whitish root vegetable (same family as the carrot)
5. a round, juicy fruit having a smooth skin and a stone or pit
6. a large, juicy fruit that grows on a vine (e.g., cantaloupe)
7. a type of peach having no fuzz on its skin
8. a long, slippery fish shaped like a snake
9. a kind of grass (herb) popular in Thai cooking
10. a vegetable that grows on vines on the ground (e.g., pumpkin)
11. a kind of melon having sweet, green flesh and a smooth, whitish skin
12. a rather large, almost round nut with a division between its two halves
13. a vegetable with a large roundish root
14. a seasoning with a hot taste, used for meats and soups
15. a small, crisp root with red or white skin, used in salads
16. a mixture of cooked meats and potatoes finely chopped and fried
17. a thick, sweet liquid that bees make
18. kinds of sweet potatoes
19. raw vegetable dishes—lettuce, tomatoes, green peppers, cauliflower, etc.—usually served with dressings

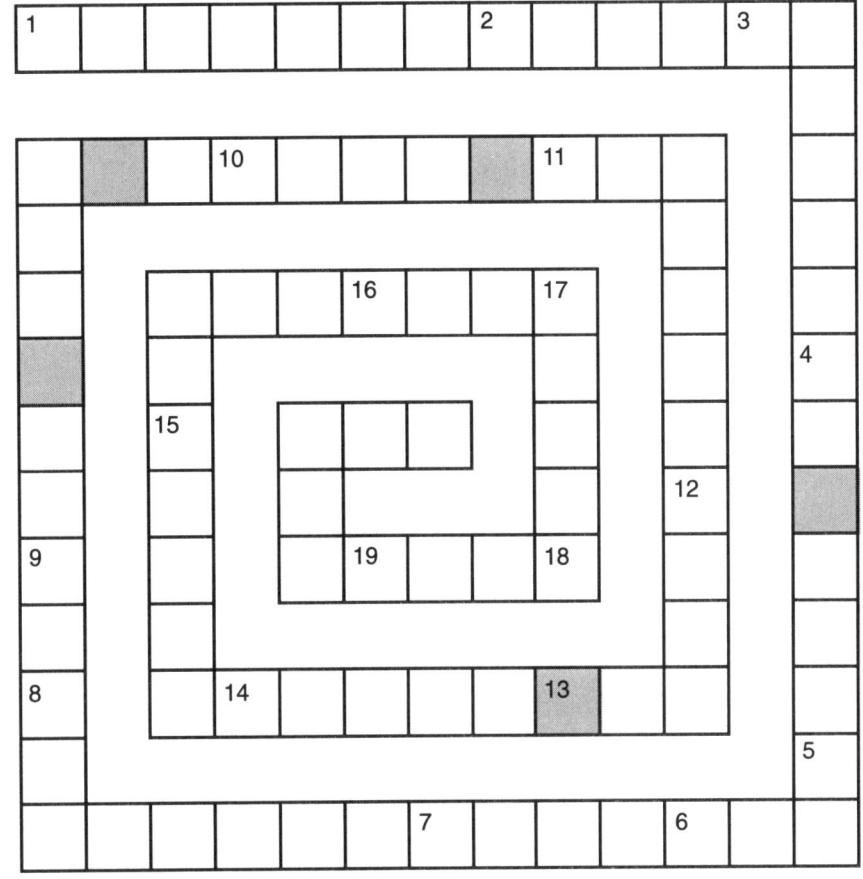

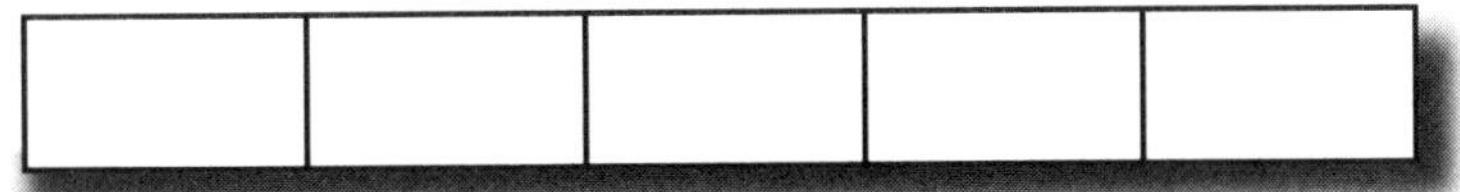

Name: ____________________ Date: ____________

Last Letter-First Letter Puzzle: *Vocabulary Development #1*

Directions: Read each clue and think of an answer. The last letter of one word will always become the first letter of the next word. To decode the puzzle, write the shaded letters (in the order they appear in the puzzle) in the boxes below. This will reveal the name of a very large, fish-eating water bird having a huge bill.

1. hard to please; never satisfied
2. period of time (12 months)
3. large animal of Africa having an upright horn(s)
4. ninth month of the year
5. open again
6. the number above the line in a fraction
7. a large farm with grazing land used for raising cattle, etc.
8. gladness; good luck
9. stamp with the foot
10. a body of still water, smaller than a lake
11. a pack of playing cards
12. a device that locks and unlocks
13. a piece of ground around the house, school, etc.
14. make a rough copy; a current of air
15. a large plant with a woody trunk, branches, and leaves
16. number that precedes 12
17. bite (not severely); pinch
18. a fear that causes one to lose self-control
19. twist or roll into coils
20. a leg or arm; a large branch
21. the forehead
22. a slender rod or stick that a magician might use
23. a wall built to hold back the water of a river

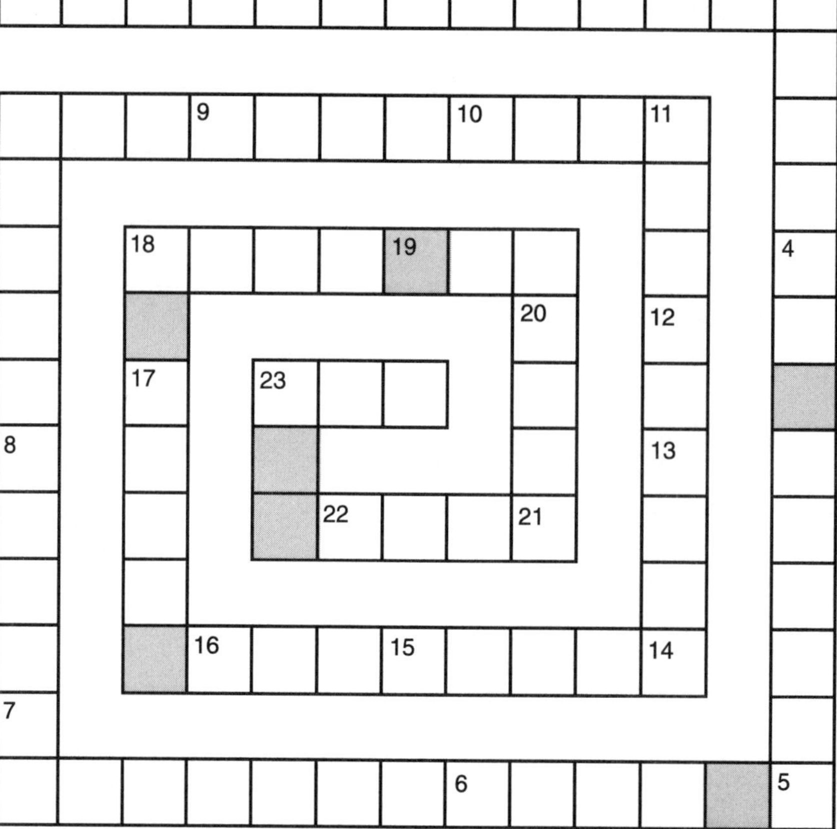

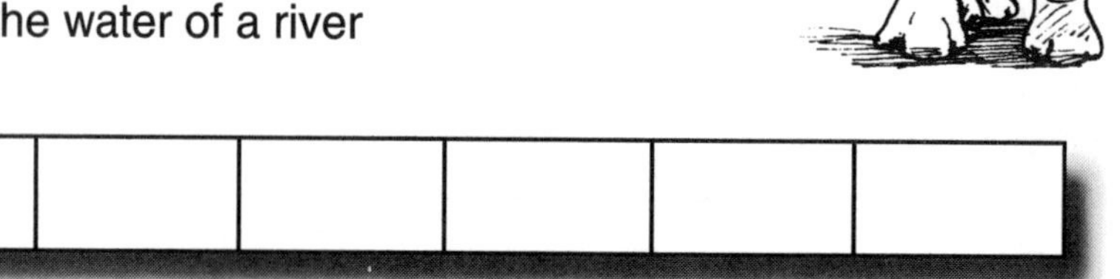

Name: ______________________________ Date: ________________

Last Letter-First Letter Puzzle: *Vocabulary Development #2*

Directions: Read each clue and think of an answer. The last letter of one word will always become the first letter of the next word. To decode the puzzle, write the shaded letters (in the order they appear in the puzzle) in the boxes below. This will reveal the name of an instrument with a pear-shaped body and metal strings played with a pick.

1. bison
2. a space in a stove for baking food
3. filthy; disgustingly dirty
4. a form of singing in the Swiss mountains
5. timber cut as logs, beams, boards, etc.
6. to wrinkle or ripple
7. to throw out; turn out
8. a large, hairy spider whose bite is painful
9. worshipped; loved
10. moisture that collects in small drops during the night
11. a woman believed to have magical powers
12. great courage; a very brave act
13. an instrument used for washing floors
14. an open pie made of bread dough and covered with sauce, cheese, meat, etc.
15. twisted the wrong way
16. join two pieces of metal by means of heat
17. think, feel, see, or hear during sleep
18. a dirty or untidy condition
19. make bare; take off the covering
20. a cucumber preserved in salt water and vinegar
21. the part of the body by which people hear
22. a strip of silk or satin used for trimming and tying
23. the sound that a horse makes

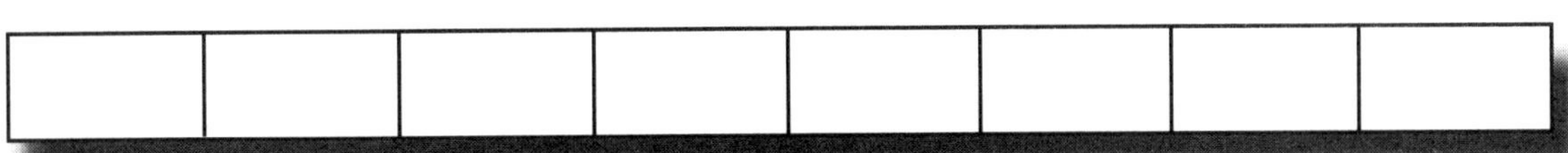

Name: ______________________________ Date: ______________

Last Letter-First Letter Puzzle: *Scrambled Words #1*

Directions: Unscramble each of the clues. The last letter of one word will always become the first letter of the next word. To decode the puzzle, write the shaded letters (in the order they appear in the puzzle) in the boxes below. This will reveal the name of a large, round, brown, hard-shelled fruit with a thick, white lining inside that is good to eat.

1. LASTB
2. OOTTTA
3. NCAEO
4. KECN
5. PELK
6. NENYP
7. TASEY
8. OXTIN
9. LENCIK
10. SRELBOT
11. GORHU
12. VIEHS
13. PMULS
14. SIPMR
15. KMLI
16. LNETK
17. OUTTR
18. MEETLP
19. VEIL
20. LAEP
21. HARAOHP
22. ERDH
23. ABD
24. ATTELB

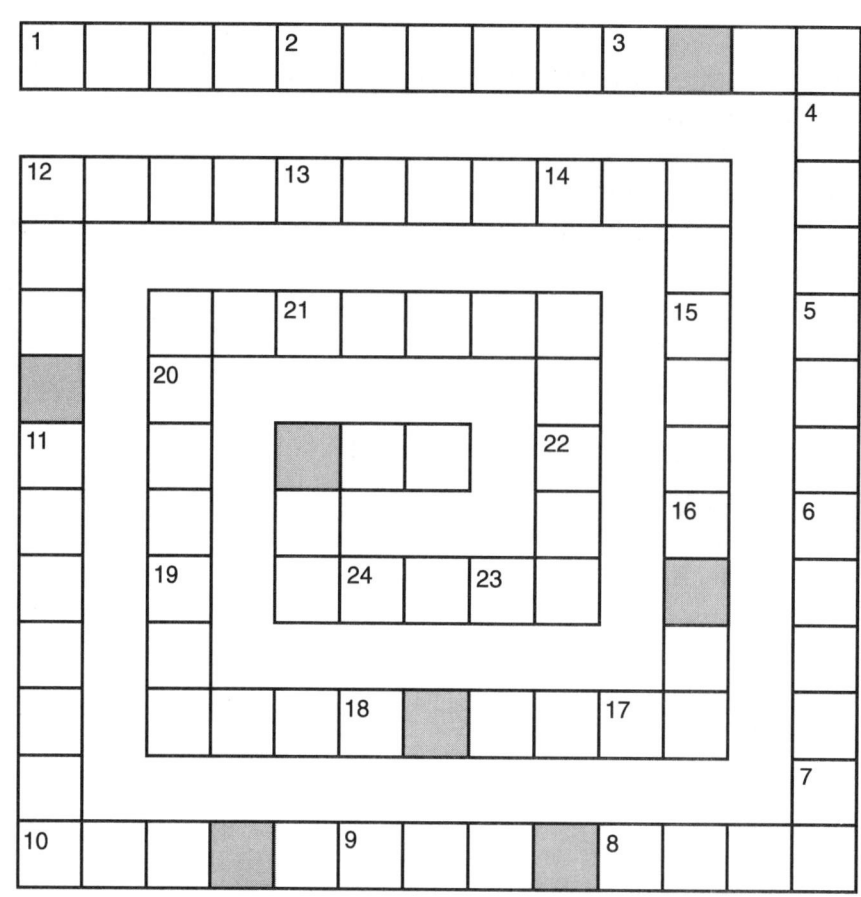

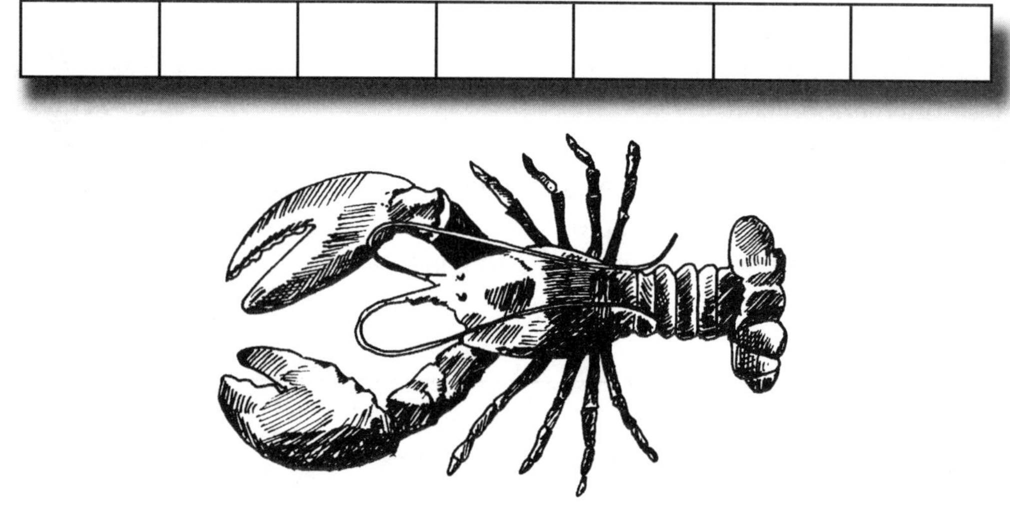

Name: ______________________________ Date: ____________________

Last Letter-First Letter Puzzle: *Scrambled Words #2*

Directions: Unscramble each of the clues. The last letter of one word will always become the first letter of the next word. To decode the puzzle, write the shaded letters (in the order they appear in the puzzle) in the boxes below. This will reveal the name of a system of writing and printing for blind people.

1. NOIL
2. LIMBEN
3. YEENM
4. CATYH
5. PERTEM
6. GORUH
7. SEHRO
8. PUEIQ
9. DOPUN
10. RAMED
11. STYYMRE
12. HOUTY
13. TORSIHCI
14. LECAST
15. BELLYEA
16. BALLUY
17. RUGTOY
18. MOBT
19. ORRUB
20. STOUTCA
21. STEO

Name: ______________________________ Date: ______________

Reveal a Palindrome: *Missing Links #1*

Palindromes can be numbers, words, or sentences that can be read from left to right and also from right to left. The following are just some examples of palindrome words: *radar*, *mom*, and *kayak*.

Directions: In this challenge you are required to find the missing letter to complete each five-letter word. Some words may have more than one possible solution; however, you must find the correct letter that can be applied to the palindrome sentence below. The number inside each box indicates where your letters are to be written. When you have decoded the palindrome, you will know what the cat lover said to her houseguest. Remember to read the answer from right to left, as well as from left to right!

MO	8 *P*	ED	GR	9	ED	PR	1	BE
ST	12	AK	HO	2	EY	PI	6	ER
FI	4	TS	LO	5	SE	RA	11	GE
BO	10	CH	PO	3	TS	WA	7	CH

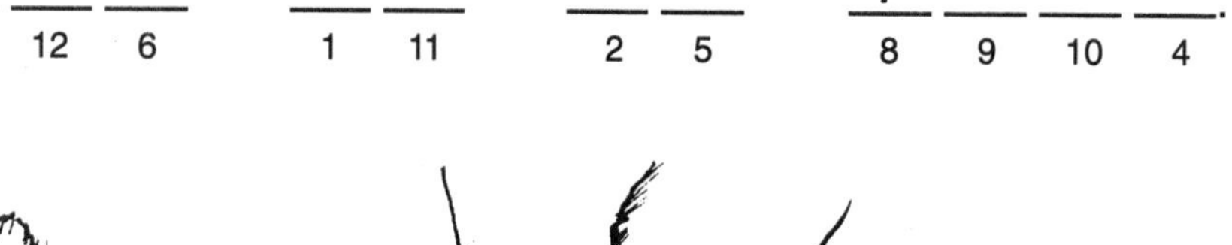

Name: ______________________________ Date: ________________

Reveal a Palindrome: *Missing Links #2*

Palindromes can be numbers, words, or sentences that can be read from left to right and also from right to left. The following are just some examples of palindrome words: *radar*, *mom*, and *kayak*.

Directions: In this challenge you are required to find the missing letter to complete each five-letter word. Some words may have more than one possible solution; however, you must find the correct letter that can be applied to the palindrome sentence below. The number inside each box indicates where your letters are to be written. When you have decoded the palindrome, you will learn what the person asked when something went speeding by. Remember to read the answer from right to left, as well as from left to right!

	Box	
AL	16	GN
AR	3	ON
BU	7	KS
CL	18	IM
CO	19	ER
DR	8	NK

	Box	
EX	5	OL
GL	12	SS
GR	10	SS
HE	6	RD
LA	11	GE
MA	9	CH
SA	17	SY

	Box	
SP	2	NK
ST	4	LE
TA	1	NY
TI	15	LE
TR	14	CK
WI	13	KS

___ ___ ___   ___ ___   ___   ___ ___ ___   ___ ___   ___   ___ ___ ___   ___
1 2 3   4 5   6   7 8 9   10 11   12   13 14 15   16

___ ___ ___?
17 18 19

Name: ______________________________ Date: ________________

Reveal a Palindrome: *Missing Links #3*

Palindromes can be numbers, words, or sentences that can be read from left to right and also from right to left. The following are just some examples of palindrome words: *radar*, *mom*, and *kayak*.

Directions: In this challenge you are required to find the missing letter to complete each five-letter word. Some words may have more than one possible solution; however, you must find the correct letter that can be applied to the palindrome sentence below. The number inside each box indicates where your letters are to be written. When you have decoded the palindrome, you will learn the name of a passageway that connects the Atlantic and Pacific Oceans. Remember to read the answer from right to left, as well as from left to right!

BL	14	ND	KN	17	VE	RE	4	TS
BR	5	SH	LI	20	BO	RE	6	LY
CH	1	SE	MA	15	LS	SA	18	DY
CO	13	ES	NA	9	NY	SE	11	TS
FL	3	KE	NY	2	PH	TA	16	ES
FL	10	ME	OP	12	LS	TR	8	SH
JE	7	LY	PR	19	WN	WR	21	TH

___ ___ ___ ___, ___ ___ ___ ___ ___, ___
1 2 3 4 5 6 7 8 9 10

___ ___ ___ ___ ___ — ___ ___ ___ ___ ___ ___.
11 12 13 14 15 16 17 18 19 20 21

Name: ______________________________ Date: ____________________

Reveal a Palindrome: *Missing Links #4*

Palindromes can be numbers, words, or sentences that can be read from left to right and also from right to left. The following are just some examples of palindrome words: *radar*, *mom*, and *kayak*.

Directions: In this challenge you are required to find the missing letter to complete each five-letter word. Some words may have more than one possible solution; however, you must find the correct letter that can be applied to the palindrome sentence below. The number inside each box indicates where your letters are to be written. When you have decoded the palindrome, you will know what every tennis player dreads doing even on his or her worst day. Remember to read the answer from right to left, as well as from left to right!

	Box	
AR	20	NA
CH	6	VE
CO	17	ES
CR	2	TE
DE	13	TA
DE	19	IM
DI	5	ER

	Box	
DI	1	TY
GR	16	PE
MA	15	BA
MI	3	CE
MU	12	IC
NO	10	EY
PI	9	OT

	Box	
PI	21	HY
QU	11	TE
RO	18	CH
SA	7	BA
SL	8	PS
SP	4	CE
TR	14	SH

___ ___ ___   ___ ___ ___ ___ ___ ___ ___   ___
1 2 3   4 5 6 7 8 9 10   11

___ ___ ___ ___   ___ ___   ___   ___ ___ ___.
12 13 14 15   16 17   18   19 20 21

Name: ______________________________ Date: ____________________

Reveal a Palindrome: *Missing Links #5*

Palindromes can be numbers, words, or sentences that can be read from left to right and also from right to left. The following are just some examples of palindrome words: *radar*, *mom*, and *kayak*.

Directions: In this challenge you are required to find the missing letter to complete each five-letter word. Some words may have more than one possible solution; however, you must find the correct letter that can be applied to the palindrome sentence below. The number inside each box indicates where your letters are to be written. When you have decoded the palindrome, you will know what the young lady said to her male suitor. Remember to read the answer from right to left, as well as from left to right!

	Box	
AL	13	GN
BA	4	KS
BR	10	WN
BU	11	PY
CO	3	ER
FL	5	SH

	Box	
GR	18	SS
GR	2	VE
IN	16	ER
MA	19	OR
ME	14	AL
MO	6	ES
QU	7	TE

	Box	
RO	9	EO
RO	17	ER
SH	12	DE
SP	8	TE
ST	15	LE
TI	1	ES

___ ___ ___, ___ ___ ___, ___ ___ ___ ___ ___ ___ ___ ___ ___ ___ ___
1 2 3 4 5 6 7 8 9 10 11 12 13 14 15 16

___ ___ ___.
17 18 19

Name: ____ Date: ____________________

Reveal a Palindrome: *Missing Links #6*

Palindromes can be numbers, words, or sentences that can be read from left to right and also from right to left. The following are just some examples of palindrome words: *radar*, *mom*, and *kayak*.

Directions: In this challenge you are required to find the missing letter to complete each five-letter word. Some words may have more than one possible solution; however, you must find the correct letter that can be applied to the palindrome sentence below. The number inside each box indicates where your letters are to be written. When you have decoded the palindrome, you will know what the speaker wanted. Remember to read the answer from right to left, as well as from left to right!

CE	8	SE	PA	2	ES	SE	17	SE
CE	18	AR	PE	10	RY	SI	11	EN
CR	12	FT	PE	19	NY	SO	4	AS
DR	14	FT	RA	15	IO	SP	3	RE
EL	9	OW	RI	5	SE	ST	16	NE
FI	13	ER	SC	1	LE	TE	20	SE
LI	7	HO	SC	6	NE	WR	21	TH

___ ___ ___ ___, ___ ___ ___ ___ ___ ___ ___: ___ ___ ___ ___ ___ ___,
1 2 3 4 5 6 7 8 9 10 11 12 13 14 15 16 17

___ ___ ___ ___.
18 19 20 21

Name: ______________________________ Date: ______________

Reveal a Palindrome: *Missing Links #7*

Palindromes can be numbers, words, or sentences that can be read from left to right and also from right to left. The following are just some examples of palindrome words: *radar*, *mom*, and *kayak*.

Directions: In this challenge you are required to find the missing letter to complete each five-letter word. Some words may have more than one possible solution; however, you must find the correct letter that can be applied to the palindrome sentence below. The number inside each box indicates where your letters are to be written. When you have decoded the palindrome, you will know why the speaker is so puzzled. Remember to read the answer from right to left, as well as from left to right!

BA	5	HE	FL	2	ME	MI	11	ER
BO	21	EL	FL	6	CK	PA	3	TE
CR	14	MP	GR	18	ND	PI	15	OT
CR	9	OK	GR	13	SS	TI	10	AN
DR	8	VE	LA	17	HE	TI	12	HE
EA	19	EL	LO	1	ER	TR	4	CK
EM	16	RY	MA	7	ES	WH	20	LE

___ ___ ___   ___ ___   ___ ___ ___ ___ ___ ' ___   ___ ___ ___ ___ ___ ___   ___

1 2 3   4 5   6 7 8 9 10 11   12 13 14 15 16 17   18

___ ___ ___?

19 20 21

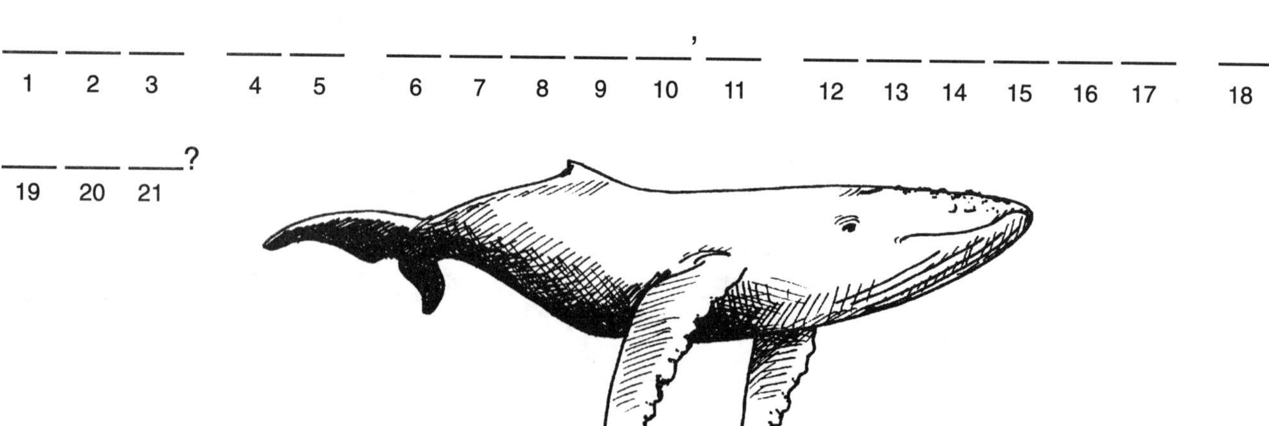

Name: ____________________ Date: ____________

Reveal a Palindrome: *Missing Links #8*

Palindromes can be numbers, words, or sentences that can be read from left to right and also from right to left. The following are just some examples of palindrome words: *radar*, *mom*, and *kayak*.

Directions: In this challenge you are required to find the missing letter to complete each five-letter word. Some words may have more than one possible solution; however, you must find the correct letter that can be applied to the palindrome sentence below. The number inside each box indicates where your letters are to be written. When you have decoded the palindrome, you will learn something about etiquette. Remember to read the answer from right to left, as well as from left to right!

AR	7	MA
CH	11	PS
CO	14	ES
FR	9	SH
GR	2	ND
GR	13	VE

LA	10	GE
MA	4	OR
PE	8	KY
PO	15	ER
RE	12	IT

RH	17	ME
SC	5	PE
SM	16	LL
SO	3	ED
TE	6	PO
TR	1	ST

___ ___ ___ ___   ___   ___ ___ ___ ___
1 2 3 4   5   6 7 8 9

___ ___ ___ ___ ___   ___ ___ ___.
10 11 12 13 14   15 16 17

Name: ______________________________ Date: ______________

Fewer Clues: *Build Your Vocabulary More #1*

Directions: Read each clue and think of an answer. The number in parentheses in front of the clue tells you how many letters are in the answer. Write your answer on the spaces to the right of the clue. Fill in the numbered boxes with the letter from each of the clues provided and arrive at a nine-letter answer.

A

1	2	3	4	5	6	7	8	9
I	*N*					*N*		

(5) a machine with a long swinging arm for lifting heavy objects ___ ___ ___ ___ ___ (8 5 6 2 9)

(4) free from doubts; certain ___ ___ ___ ___ (3 4 5 9)

(3) a place where a traveler can get a room to sleep in *I* *N* *N* (1 2 7)

B

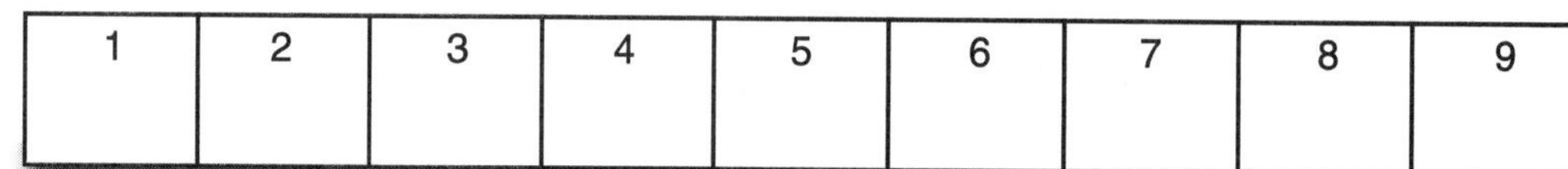

1	2	3	4	5	6	7	8	9

(4) a story; a falsehood or lie ___ ___ ___ ___ (4 8 5 6)

(5) a substance that can conduct heat and can be made into wire ___ ___ ___ ___ ___ (7 6 3 2 5)

(4) the contraction for cannot ___ ___ ___ ___ (1 8 9 3)

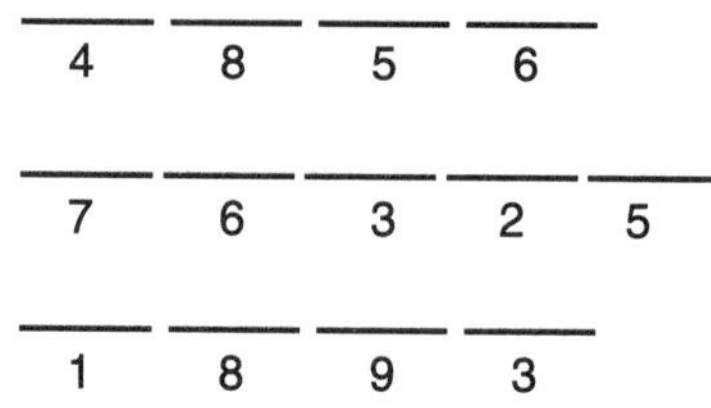

C

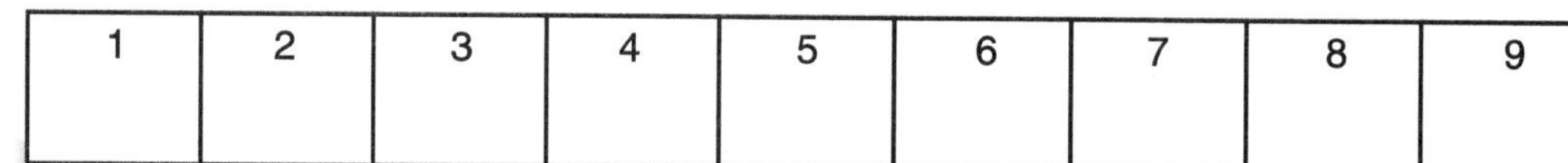

1	2	3	4	5	6	7	8	9

(5) a firm belief in the honesty or truthfulness of a person; faith ___ ___ ___ ___ ___ (9 4 8 2 3)

(4) speak wildly, violently, or noisily ___ ___ ___ ___ (4 7 6 3)

(5) a slice or slices of bread browned by heat ___ ___ ___ ___ ___ (9 5 1 2 3)

Name: ______________________________ Date: ____________________

Fewer Clues: *Build Your Vocabulary More #2*

Directions: Read each clue and think of an answer. The number in parentheses in front of the clue tells you how many letters are in the answer. Write your answer on the spaces to the right of the clue. Fill in the numbered boxes with the letter from each of the clues provided and arrive at a nine-letter answer.

1	2	3	4	5	6	7	8	9

(4) a small building used for storage ___ ___ ___ ___ (3 4 7 1)

(4) grind a cutting tool to a sharp edge ___ ___ ___ ___ (4 5 6 7)

(4) fastens with string; binds ___ ___ ___ ___ (9 2 7 8)

B

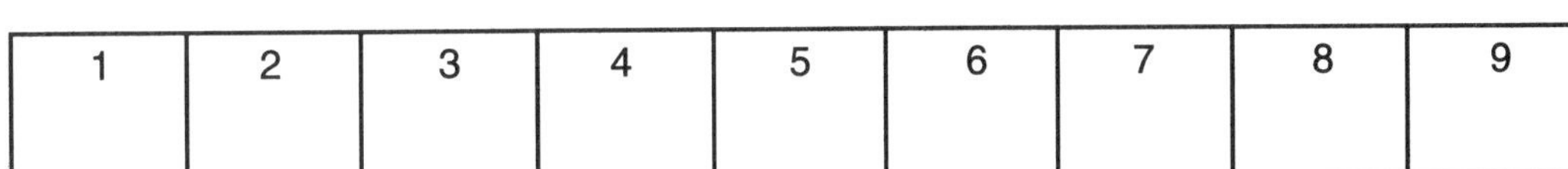

(6) the groupings of nouns (masculine, feminine, neuter) ___ ___ ___ ___ ___ ___ (3 4 5 6 2 8)

(5) big; of more than the usual size ___ ___ ___ ___ ___ (1 7 8 3 4)

(3) the time of light between sunrise and sunset ___ ___ ___ (6 7 9)

C

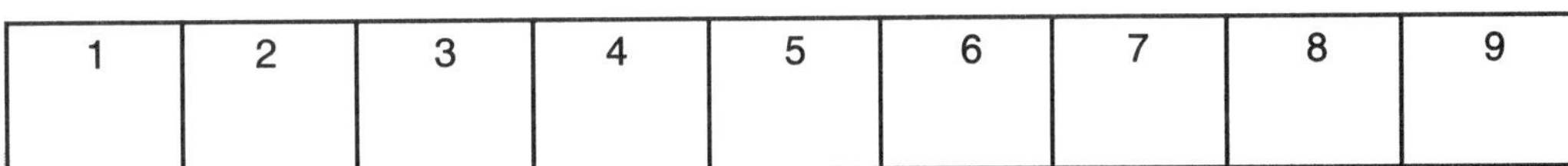

(4) a suggestion or hint ___ ___ ___ ___ (4 6 5 9)

(4) a row of words on a page ___ ___ ___ ___ (6 1 2 9)

(4) an outer garment of cloth or fur with sleeves ___ ___ ___ ___ (4 3 7 8)

Name: ____________________________________ Date: ____________________

Fewer Clues: *Build Your Vocabulary More #3*

Directions: Read each clue and think of an answer. The number in parentheses in front of the clue tells you how many letters are in the answer. Write your answer on the spaces to the right of the clue. Fill in the numbered boxes with the letter from each of the clues provided and arrive at a nine-letter answer.

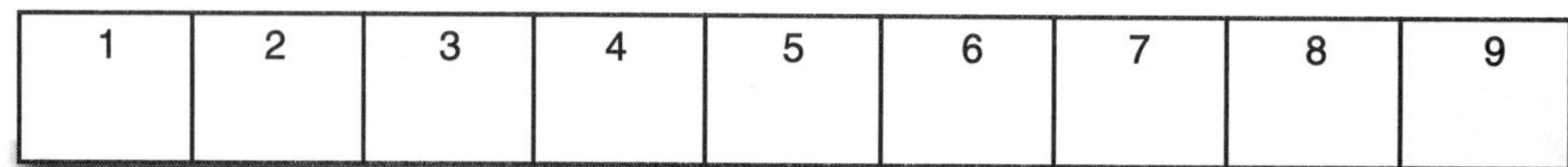

(5) provided with weapons ____ ____ ____ ____ ____
2 3 4 9 8

(4) not able to walk properly; crippled ____ ____ ____ ____
6 5 4 9

(3) crazy; insane; out of one's mind ____ ____ ____
1 7 8

B

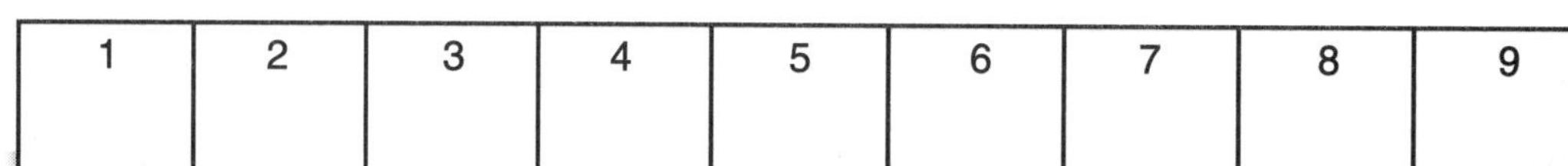

(4) sympathy; sorrow for another's suffering ____ ____ ____ ____
1 7 8 9

(4) be still or quiet; in music, a pause ____ ____ ____ ____
6 5 3 4

(6) a person who makes pottery ____ ____ ____ ____ ____ ____
1 2 4 8 5 6

C

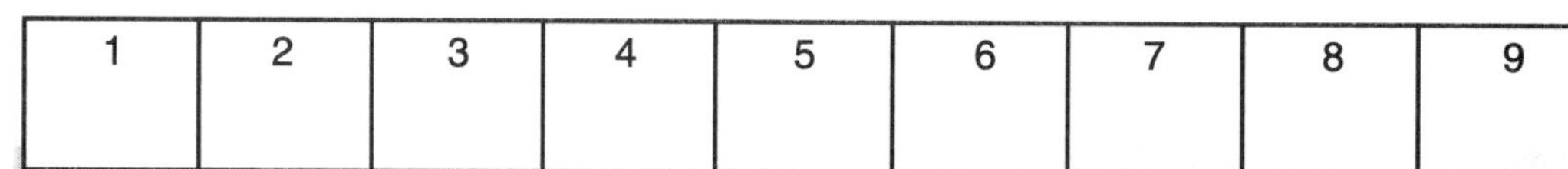

(4) walk through water or anything that hinders free motion ____ ____ ____ ____
6 4 3 9

(5) essential; very important ____ ____ ____ ____ ____
8 2 1 7 5

(4) disk on a radio with numbers on it for tuning in a station ____ ____ ____ ____
3 2 4 5

Name: ______________________________ Date: ____________________

Fewer Clues: *Build Your Vocabulary More #4*

Directions: Read each clue and think of an answer. The number in parentheses in front of the clue tells you how many letters are in the answer. Write your answer on the spaces to the right of the clue. Fill in the numbered boxes with the letter from each of the clues provided and arrive at a nine-letter answer.

1	2	3	4	5	6	7	8	9

(5) put the hand on or against and feel ___ ___ ___ ___ ___ (3 4 5 6 7)

(4) the seed-bearing part in pine, cedar, and spruce trees ___ ___ ___ ___ (6 4 2 8)

(6) caught and killed wild animals ___ ___ ___ ___ ___ ___ (7 1 2 3 8 9)

B

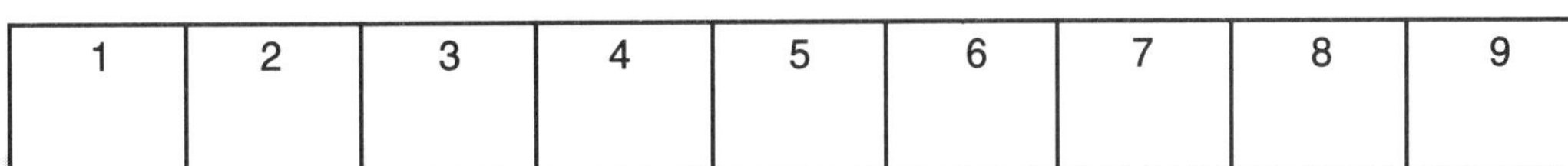

(4) a ballot ___ ___ ___ ___ (1 2 6 7)

(5) not ever; at no time ___ ___ ___ ___ ___ (5 7 1 8 9)

(4) govern; a statement of what to do and what not to do ___ ___ ___ ___ (9 4 3 7)

C

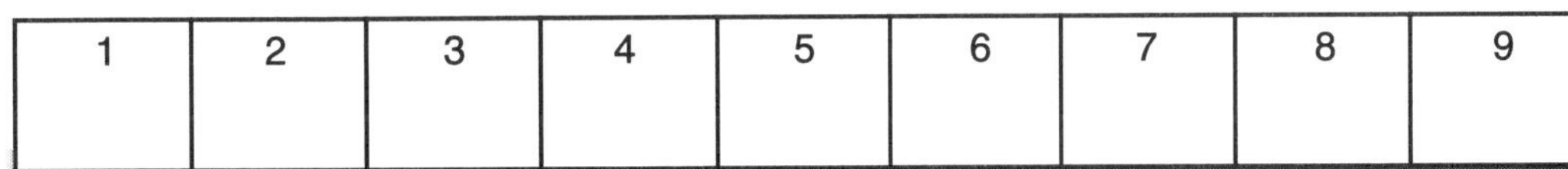

(6) a hanging bunch of threads fastened together at the top ___ ___ ___ ___ ___ ___ (4 2 3 8 7 6)

(4) selling at lower than usual price; the act of selling ___ ___ ___ ___ (9 2 6 7)

(4) opposite of early ___ ___ ___ ___ (6 2 1 5)

Name: ______________________________ Date: ______________

Fewer Clues: *Build Your Vocabulary More #5*

Directions: Read each clue and think of an answer. The number in parentheses in front of the clue tells you how many letters are in the answer. Write your answer on the spaces to the right of the clue. Fill in the numbered boxes with the letter from each of the clues provided and arrive at a nine-letter answer.

1	2	3	4	5	6	7	8	9

(4) very unpleasant; disgusting ___ ___ ___ ___ (7 6 3 2)

(4) put a value on; rank; estimate; consider ___ ___ ___ ___ (1 4 5 8)

(4) lay aside; store up (money) ___ ___ ___ ___ (9 4 7 8)

B

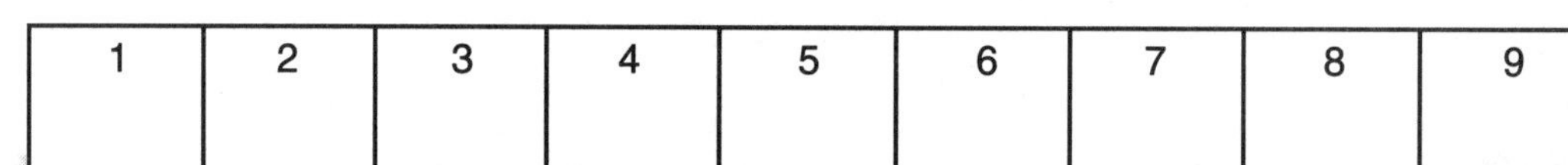

1	2	3	4	5	6	7	8	9

(5) a gift of food, drink, or amusement ___ ___ ___ ___ ___ (6 2 9 3 4)

(4) impolite; not courteous ___ ___ ___ ___ (2 7 8 9)

(4) very fine bits of sand or gravel ___ ___ ___ ___ (1 2 5 6)

C

1	2	3	4	5	6	7	8	9

(6) suffering; woe; agony ___ ___ ___ ___ ___ ___ (4 5 6 3 8 9)

(5) the clock will ring on the hour and half hour ___ ___ ___ ___ ___ (1 2 5 4 3)

(4) metropolis; municipality; town ___ ___ ___ ___ (1 5 7 9)

Name: ______________________________ Date: ____________________

Fewer Clues: *Build Your Vocabulary More #6*

Directions: Read each clue and think of an answer. The number in parentheses in front of the clue tells you how many letters are in the answer. Write your answer on the spaces to the right of the clue. Fill in the numbered boxes with the letter from each of the clues provided and arrive at a nine-letter answer.

1	2	3	4	5	6	7	8	9

Clue	Spaces
(5) a number or letter that shows how well you have done	6 4 7 9 5
(4) stand up; get up from a lying or sitting position	8 2 3 5
(4) stopped living; became dead	1 2 5 9

B

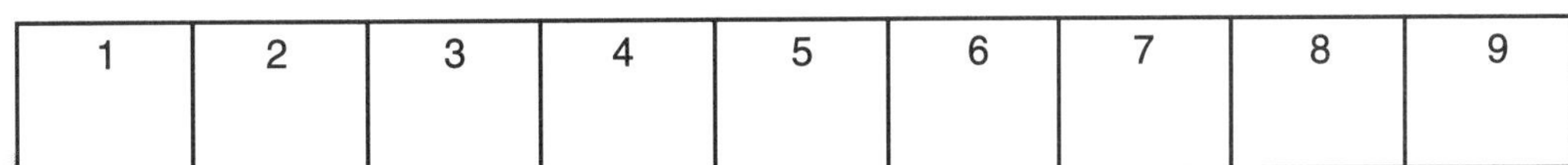

1	2	3	4	5	6	7	8	9

Clue	Spaces
(6) a drink used as a medicine or poison	2 8 6 7 1 9
(4) strong cord made of twisted fiber or wire	4 1 2 3
(4) estimate; rank; put a value on	4 5 6 3

C

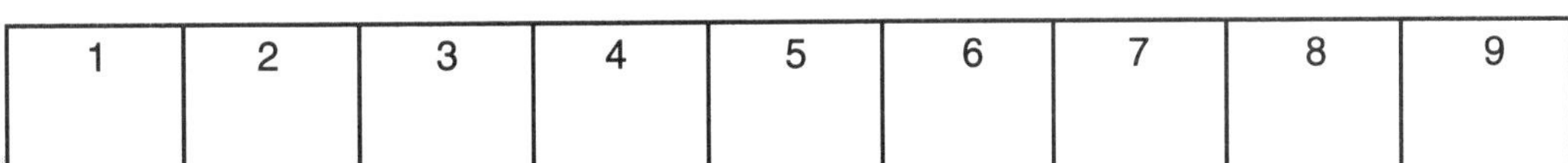

1	2	3	4	5	6	7	8	9

Clue	Spaces
(6) the mouthpiece in a baby's bottle	3 2 6 1 8 9
(4) a tube through which a liquid or gas flows	6 2 1 4
(4) without much color; whitish	7 5 8 4

Name: ______________________________ Date: ________________

Four-Squared Puzzle: *Vocabulary Enrichment #1*

Directions: Think of an answer for each clue. Write your answer in the space provided. When you have finished, decode the hidden message by reading down the shaded boxes in #1, up the shaded boxes in #2, up in #3, and down in #4. Fill in the lines at the bottom of the page with your answers.

1

F	*R*	*I*	*E*	*D*

1
2
3
4
5

2

3

1
2
3
4
5

4

1

1. cooked in hot fat
2. the direction to which a compass needle points
3. a slender shaft or stick having a pointed tip
4. very dirty; covered in grime
5. performing; completing

2

1. not easily bent
2. a large frame or box used to pack furniture, fruit, etc.
3. a male duck
4. small; having little importance or value
5. sound alike in the last part

3

1. look forward to with fear
2. rise to one's feet
3. think, feel, see, or hear during sleep
4. opposite of day
5. a large, black bird resembling a crow

4

1. without noise; quiet
2. call or cry loudly and vigorously
3. covered with hair
4. turns over quickly
5. twelve dozen; 144

F ___ ___ ___   ___ ___ ___ ___ ___ ___   ___ ___ ___ ___ ___ ___ ___ ___ ___ ___ ___.

Name: ______________________________ Date: ________________

Four-Squared Puzzle: *Vocabulary Enrichment #2*

Directions: Think of an answer for each clue. Write your answer in the space provided. When you have finished, decode the hidden message by reading down the shaded boxes in #1, up the shaded boxes in #2, up in #3, and down in #4. Fill in the lines at the bottom of the page with your answers.

1

1
2
3
4
5

2

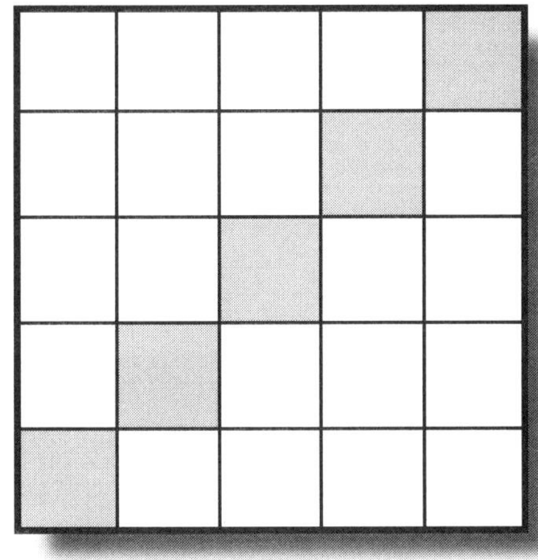

3

1
2
3
4
5

4

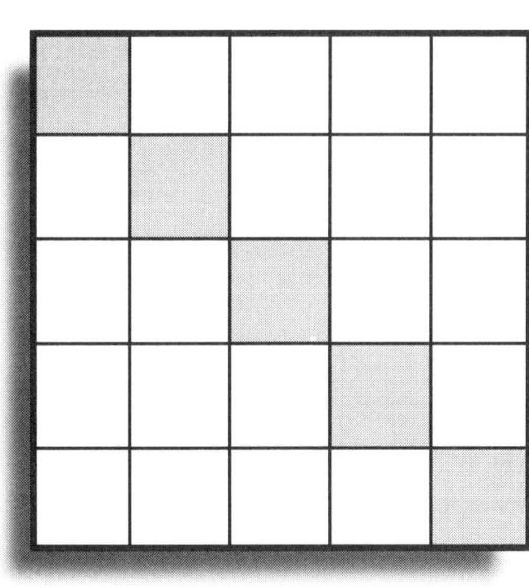

1

1. a stand for supporting a painting
2. a grown-up person
3. dull; without a sharp edge or point
4. copy by following the lines with a pencil
5. a gray, furry Australian animal that eats eucalyptus leaves

2

1. a person who feeds and takes care of horses
2. a dried sweet plum
3. an instrument for measuring and showing time
4. the book of sacred writings of the Christian religion
5. of food or drink, tasting good

3

1. the yellowish part of milk that contains fat
2. the land along the sea; seashore
3. to lose blood
4. the bones of the head
5. the nut of an oak tree

4

1. run away to get married
2. faint
3. a steep, high face of rock
4. a yellow metal made of copper and zinc
5. opposite of open

_ _ _ _ _ _ _ _ _   _ _ _ _ _   _ _   _ _ _ _.

Name: ______________________________ Date: ______________

Four-Squared Puzzle: *Vocabulary Enrichment #3*

Directions: Think of an answer for each clue. Write your answer in the space provided. When you have finished, decode the hidden message by reading down the shaded boxes in #1, up the shaded boxes in #2, up in #3, and down in #4. Fill in the lines at the bottom of the page with your answers.

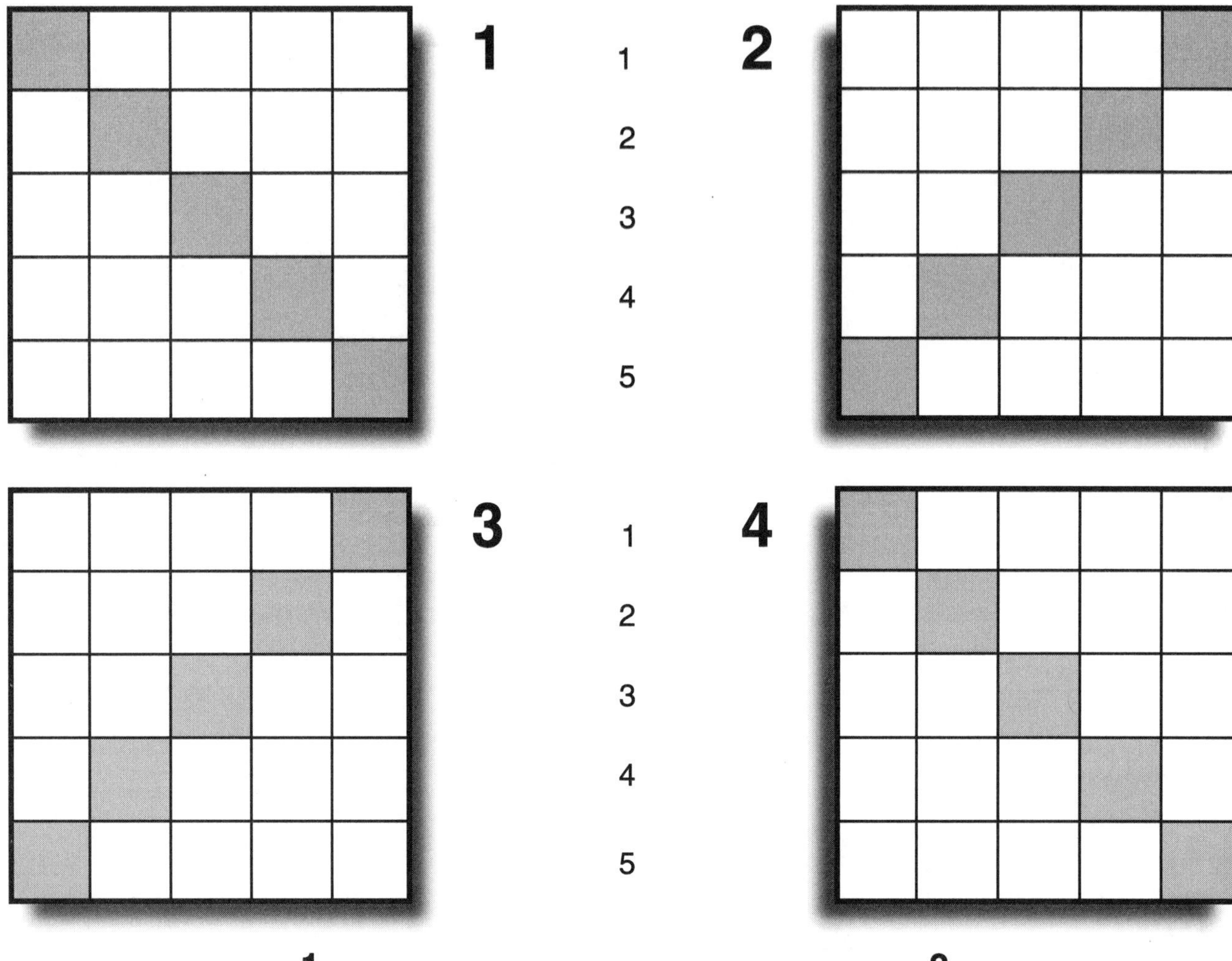

1

1. tired; causing tiredness
2. buffalo
3. a person whose work is building with stone or brick
4. buy and sell; exchange goods
5. a game in which players cover numbers on a card as they are called out

2

1. a seat hung from ropes in which one sits and moves back and forth
2. like the moon
3. go to see; make a call on
4. a tree having light-colored bark that peels easily
5. make fun of by imitating

3

1. an older person
2. a deep passage as in a mine
3. go into; come into; enroll
4. later; following
5. a list at the end of a book with topics and page numbers

4

1. happen; take place
2. change for the better
3. feeling of wanting to get back at a person who wrongs you
4. past tense of stand
5. a flow of water over what is usually dry land

__ __ __ __ __ __   __ __   __   __ __ __ __   __ __ __ __

__ __ __.

Name: ______________________ Date: ______________

Four-Squared Puzzle: *Vocabulary Enrichment #4*

Directions: Think of an answer for each clue. Write your answer in the space provided. When you have finished, decode the hidden message by reading down the shaded boxes in #1, up the shaded boxes in #2, up in #3, and down in #4. Fill in the lines at the bottom of the page with your answers.

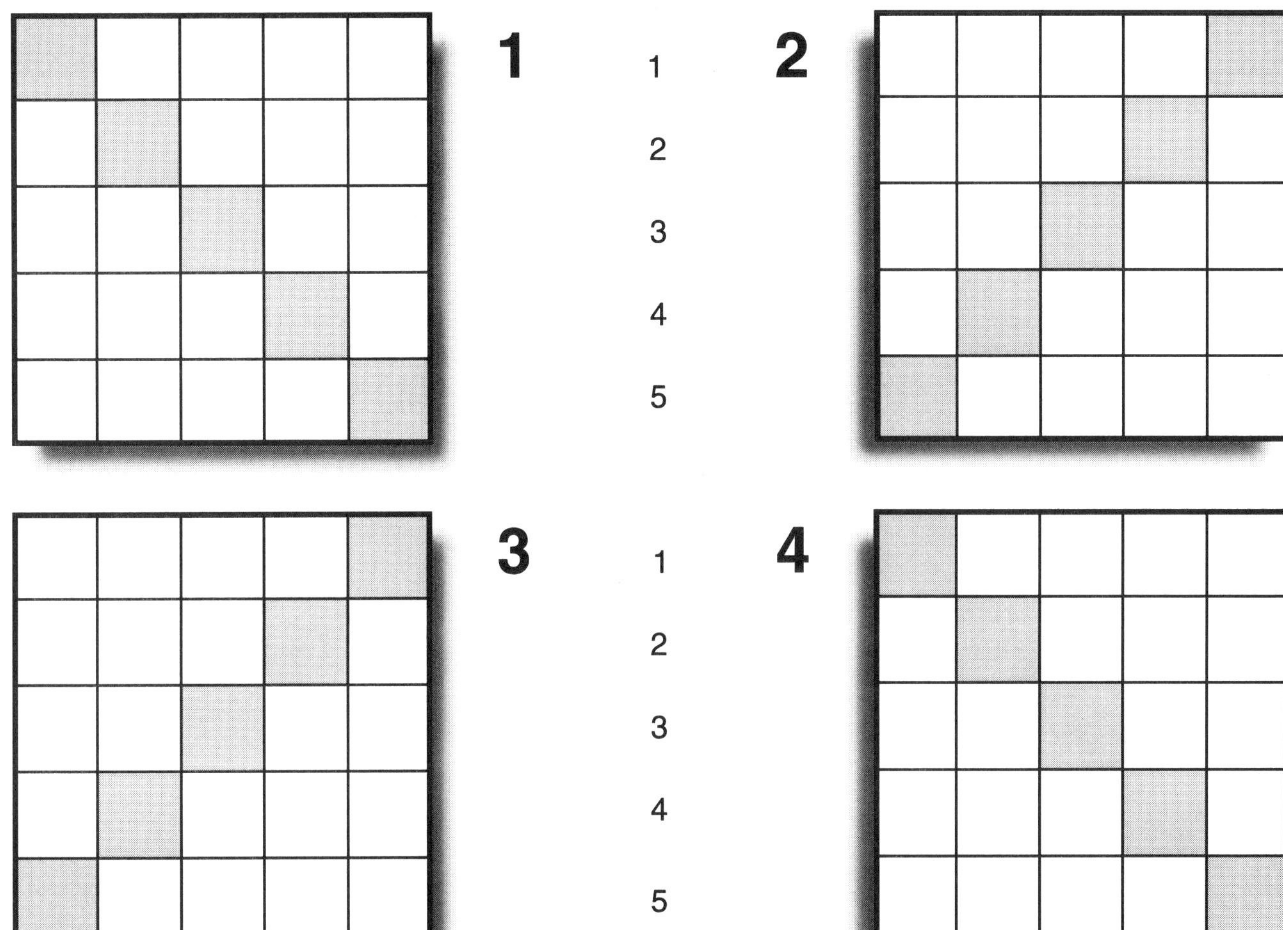

1

1. seaweeds and certain freshwater plants
2. bicycles
3. kept track of the time
4. fill a chicken or turkey with dressing
5. one of a pair of small, connected drums that are played with the hands

2

1. beat rapidly or strongly, like a pulse
2. crawl; move in a slow and stealthy way
3. a person who shows people to their seats in a theater
4. a book of maps
5. very quick; swift

3

1. a woman about to be married
2. watchful; wide awake
3. be alike; go well together
4. something of value
5. throw out; drive out

4

1. draw air through the nose in quick breaths that can be heard
2. a light meal between breakfast and dinner
3. bravery; courage
4. six times ten
5. the green plants that cover fields, lawns, and pastures

___ ___ ___   ___ ___ ___   ___ ___ ___   ___ ___ ___ ___

___ ___ ___ ___ ___ ___ ___.

Name: ______________________________ Date: ______________

Four-Squared Puzzle: *Vocabulary Enrichment #5*

Directions: Think of an answer for each clue. Write your answer in the space provided. When you have finished, decode the hidden message by reading down the shaded boxes in #1, up the shaded boxes in #2, up in #3, and down in #4. Fill in the lines at the bottom of the page with your answers.

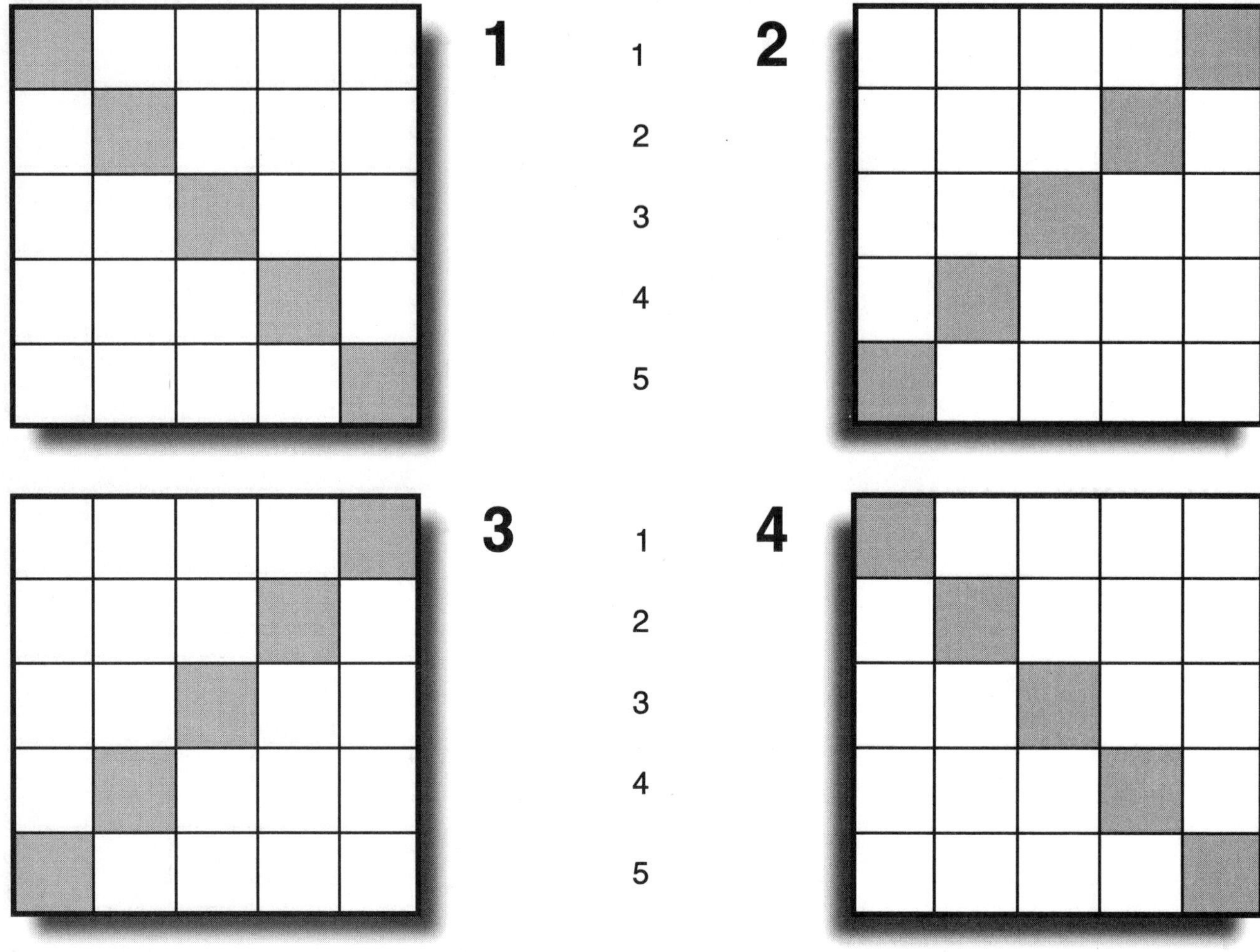

1

1. dark; gloomy
2. part of the body between the ribs and the hips
3. a person who makes or sells bread or pies
4. to get down on one's knee(s)
5. to be held up by air or water

2

1. having to do with sound
2. make a grinding sound; sound harshly
3. very poor; not having enough to live on
4. leaves out
5. a hard, white substance composing the tusks of elephants

3

1. rough; rude; unfriendly
2. (informal) a close friend; pal; comrade
3. daily journal
4. gain knowledge or skill; memorize
5. respond or answer

4

1. one who owns
2. firm and stiff but breaking or snapping easily
3. propose; suggest; be willing
4. a number of persons together
5. one who worships more than one god; a heathen

___ ___ ___ ___ ___ ___ ___ ___ ___ ___ ___ ___ ___ ___ ___ ___ ___ ___ ___

___ ___ ___.

Name: ______________________________ Date: ______________

Four-Squared Puzzle: *Vocabulary Enrichment #6*

Directions: Think of an answer for each clue. Write your answer in the space provided. When you have finished, decode the hidden message by reading down the shaded boxes in #1, up the shaded boxes in #2, up in #3, and down in #4. Fill in the lines at the bottom of the page with your answers.

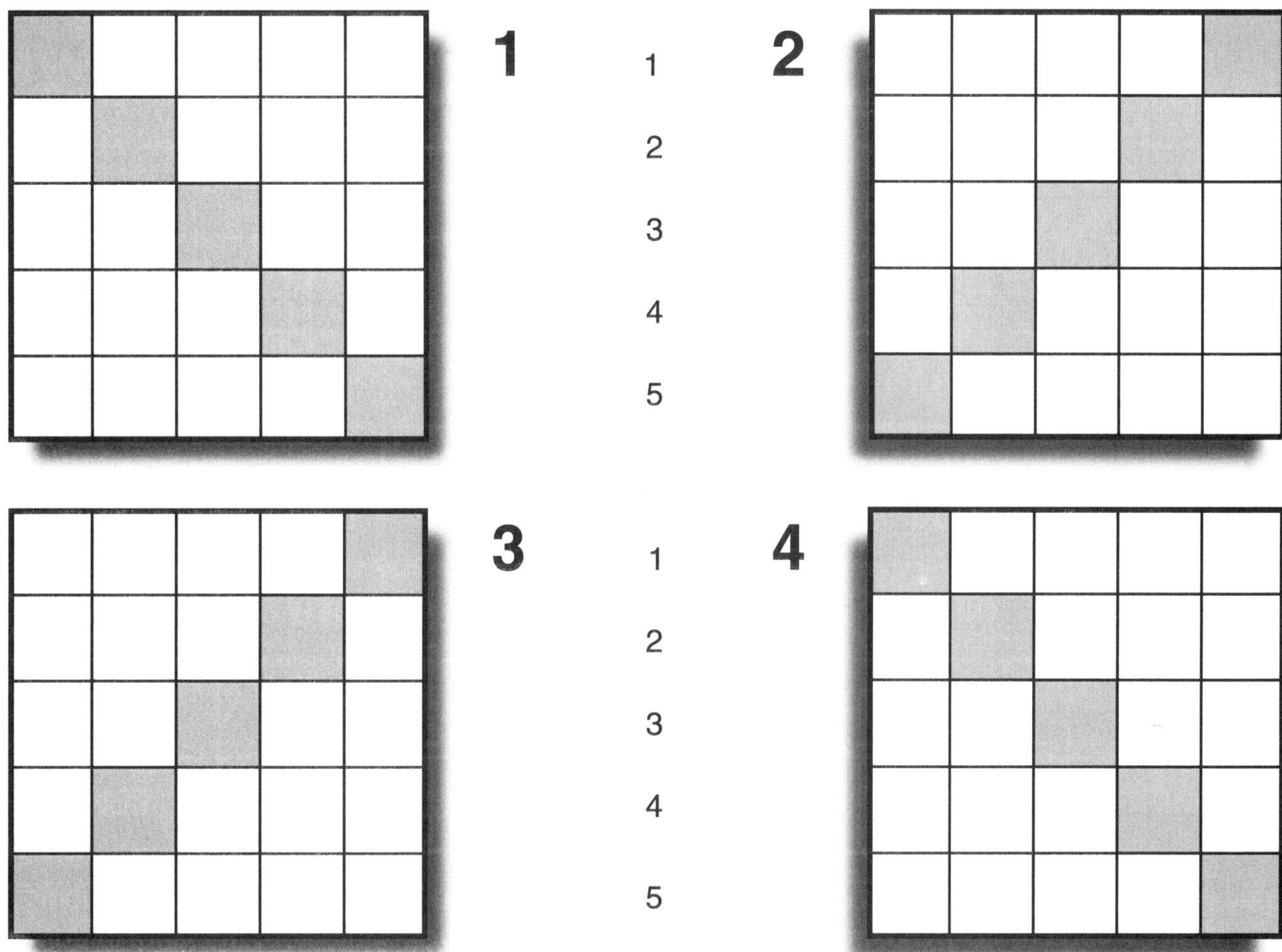

1

1. rub hard; wash or clean by rubbing
2. having a tendency to curl
3. laps up with the tongue
4. songbird having a short, strong bill
5. a small, round fruit that grows in bunches on vines

2

1. water in the form of vapor or gas
2. a vegetable with a sharp, strong smell and taste
3. the common part of *bicycle, tricycle,* and *motorcycle*
4. a short written work on a specific subject
5. a seat without a back or arms

3

1. make a picture with coloring matter using a brush
2. the art of putting sounds together in interesting arrangements
3. soft as down; fluffy
4. in common use; ordinary
5. the joint between the upper arm and forearm

4

1. plants used for seasonings or food
2. not asleep
3. a dwarf supposed to live on Earth to guard treasures
4. keep from escaping
5. horrify; amaze

___ ___ ___ ___ ___ ___ ___   ___ ___ ___ ___ ___   ___ ___ ___ ___   ___ ___ ___ ___.

Name: ______________________________ Date: ____________________

Back and Forth Puzzle: *Unusual Vocabulary Challenge #1*

Directions: Read the clues carefully and print your answer in the appropriate boxes. The last three letters of answer #1 become the first three letters of answer #2 and so on. (All of the even-numbered answers read from right to left.)

1	*M*	*O*	*R*
3	*R*	*E*	*S*
5			
7			
9			
11			
13			
15			
17			
19			
21			
23			
25			

S	*E*	*L*	2
			4
			6
			8
			10
			12
			14
			16
			18
			20
			22
			24

1-2. A small bite; piece or fragment
2-3. Smaller; the least important of two
3-4. To absorb again
4-5. A professional who works in the stock market
5-6. Undo and knit again
6-7. A miner who works in a tin mine; tinsmith
7-8. Anything used to curdle milk
8-9. A sport using a racket
9-10. One who makes music with the voice
10-11. Feel sorry for or about; sorrow
11-12. Metal ring on a horse's harness (a rein passes through it)
12-13. Worded in a more concise and succinct way
13-14. A place people visit for rest or recreation
14-15. A sharp surgical instrument used to drain fluid
15-16. An unbranched flower cluster
16-17. To rise from; to become visible
17-18. A type of heron (plural)
18-19. To stow cargo in the hold of a ship
19-20. Made even
20-21. Bent or damaged
21-22. Keep from going ahead; hold back
22-23. A vitamin
23-24. Superlative form of nice
24-25. An African fly

Name: ______________________________ Date: ______________

Back and Forth Puzzle: *Unusual Vocabulary Challenge #2*

Directions: Read the clues carefully and print your answer in the appropriate boxes. The last three letters of answer #1 become the first three letters of answer #2 and so on. (All of the even-numbered answers read from right to left.)

1							
							2
3							
							4
5							
							6
7							
							8
9							
							10
11							
							12
13							
							14
15							
							16
17							
							18
19							
							20
21							
							22
23							
							24
25							

1-2. Soldiers
2-3. Games or contests requiring skills
3-4. A badge or symbol of rank (in the armed services)
4-5. A concluding part added to a book
5-6. Played a game with a ball and various clubs
6-7. Resisted boldly or openly
7-8. The smaller of the two moons of Mars
8-9. Dark and gloomy; solemn
9-10. People who resist government or authority
10-11. Rests the body and mind at night
11-12. Gushed forth; vomited
12-13. Loose flap of skin that hangs from the neck of a cow
13-14. Platform on which materials are stacked
14-15. A bank clerk
15-16. Laid again
16-17. A crown; something resembling a crown
17-18. Middle; intermediate
18-19. Fastened together with nails
19-20. Of extra fine quality; luxurious
20-21. Seems to radiate or ooze
21-22. Automobiles with front and back seats
22-23. Traps for small animals
23-24. A waiter or waitress
24-25. Increased the number of r.p.m.'s (of an engine)

Name: ______________________________ Date: ______________

Back and Forth Puzzle: *Unusual Vocabulary Challenge #3*

Directions: Read the clues carefully and print your answer in the appropriate boxes. The last three letters of answer #1 become the first three letters of answer #2 and so on. (All of the even-numbered answers read from right to left.)

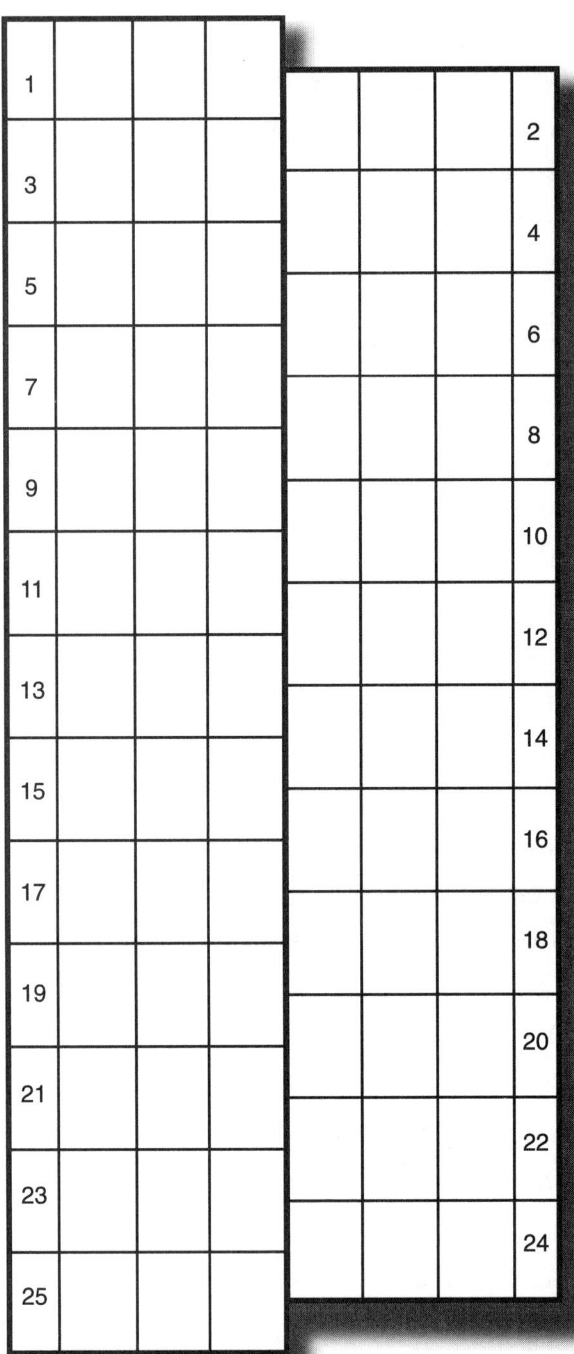

1-2. Neat; trim; smartly dressed

2-3. To mend; to fix; to put in good condition

3-4. Lariats; lassos (Spanish)

4-5. Money used in Thailand

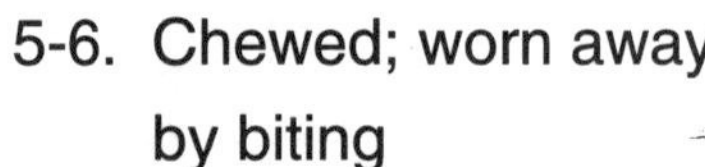

5-6. Chewed; worn away by biting

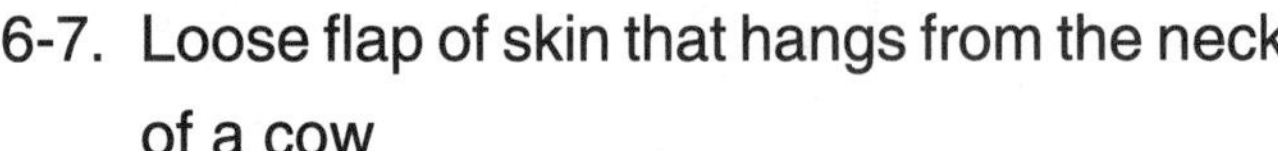

6-7. Loose flap of skin that hangs from the neck of a cow

7-8. Paleness; lack of color from fear or illness

8-9. Moved along by turning over and over

9-10. Places earth is deposited at the mouths of rivers

10-11. Governor of a province in ancient Persia

11-12. Brightly-colored tropical bird

12-13. Dormant; sluggish; dull

13-14. Dunked into a liquid and quickly taken out

14-15. To leave

15-16. Paths where people or animals walk

16-17 Splinter; long, thin piece of wood

17-18. Takes great pleasure in merrymaking

18-19. Part of a garment that covers the arm

19-20. Turns inside out

20-21. A symbol of rank in the armed services

21-22. A concluding part added to a book

22-23. Played a game with a ball and various clubs

23-24. Make dirty or disgusting in any way

24-25. To arrive at (the truth) by questioning

Name: ______________________________ Date: ________________

Back and Forth Puzzle: *Unusual Vocabulary Challenge #4*

Directions: Read the clues carefully and print your answer in the appropriate boxes. The last three letters of answer #1 become the first three letters of answer #2 and so on. (All of the even-numbered answers read from right to left.)

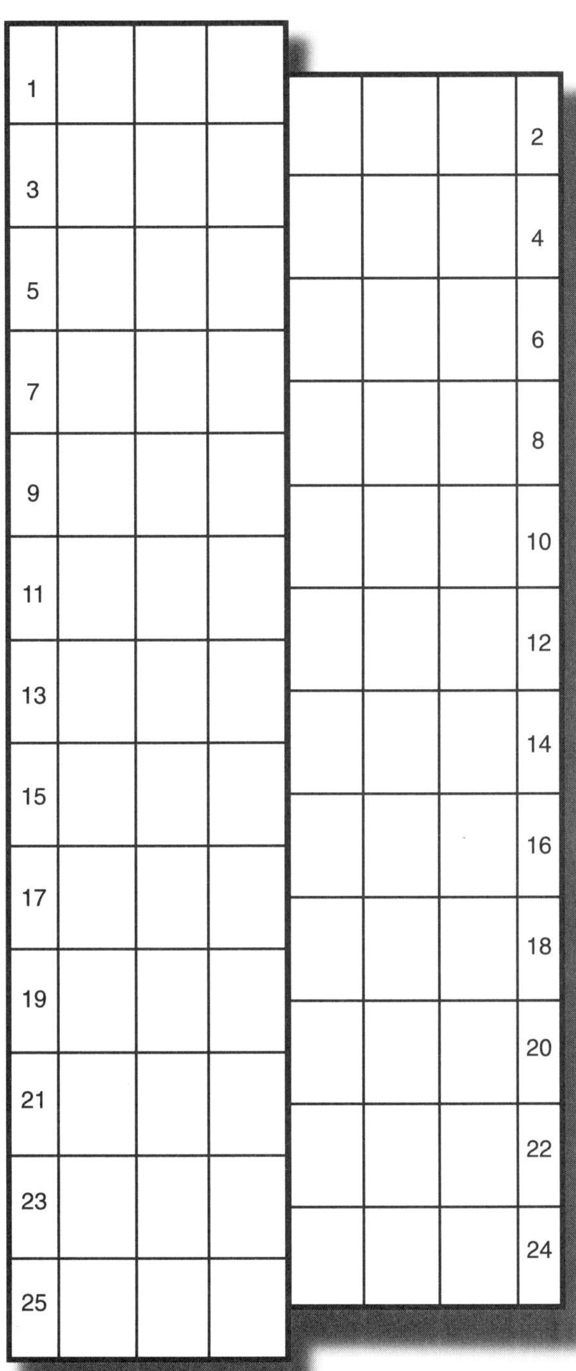

1-2. To boil gently
2-3. A written or spoken comment
3-4. Enclosures for cattle or sheep (Afrikaans)
4-5. A person involved in the slave trade
5-6. Go back; return
6-7. Three times; the highest part in music
7-8. Joints between upper arms and forearms
8-9. Faints
9-10. Breathed during sleep with a harsh sound
10-11. Woody, climbing plants of the East Indies
11-12. Devices producing loud wailing sounds
12-13. Moves in a stealthy, sly way
13-14. Glides on ice
14-15. A person who sets or arranges things
15-16. Reply quickly or sharply
16-17. Bands of Boy Scouts; soldiers
17-18. Eating utensils with shallow bowls
18-19. Past tense of snow
19-20. Loose skin that hangs from the neck of a cow
20-21. Wooden platform on which goods are stacked
21-22. Cashier in a bank
22-23. Artifacts from the past
23-24. Descendants of noble families
24-25. Goes about in a sneaking, prying way

Name: ______________________________ Date: ______________

Back and Forth Puzzle: *Unusual Vocabulary Challenge #5*

Directions: Read the clues carefully and print your answer in the appropriate boxes. The last three letters of answer #1 become the first three letters of answer #2 and so on. (All of the even-numbered answers read from right to left.)

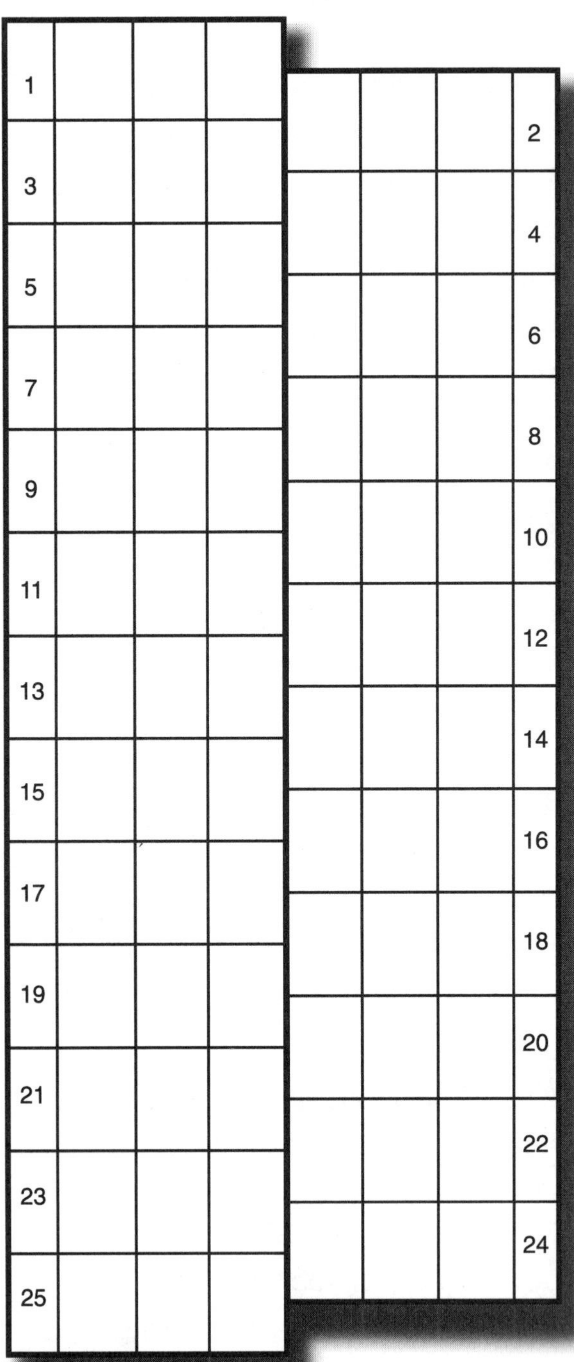

1-2. Comment; state
2-3. Large vase used for mixing wine by ancient Greeks
3-4. Reply quickly or sharply
4-5. Enlisted men; soldiers
5-6. Verbal; uttered; oral
6-7. Organisms swimming actively in water
7-8. Thought; idea; impression
8-9. Sounds; outcries
9-10. The last six lines of a sonnet
10-11. Set of four; a group of four cells
11-12. Mended by weaving yarn across a hole
12-13. Of or for the teeth
13-14. More recent; later; opposite of former
14-15. Part of the eye that receives images
15-16. Any living thing that is not a plant
16-17. Superlative form of lame
17-18. African fly
18-19. Value; high regard; revere
19-20. Comparative form of meek
20-21. Unravel and knit again
21-22. Anything that catches fire easily
22-23. Even more red than before
23-24. Term for showing a loss in one's accounts
24-25. A medieval soldier

Name: ______________________________ Date: ____________________

Back and Forth Puzzle: *Unusual Vocabulary Challenge #6*

Directions: Read the clues carefully and print your answer in the appropriate boxes. The last three letters of answer #1 become the first three letters of answer #2 and so on. (All of the even-numbered answers read from right to left.)

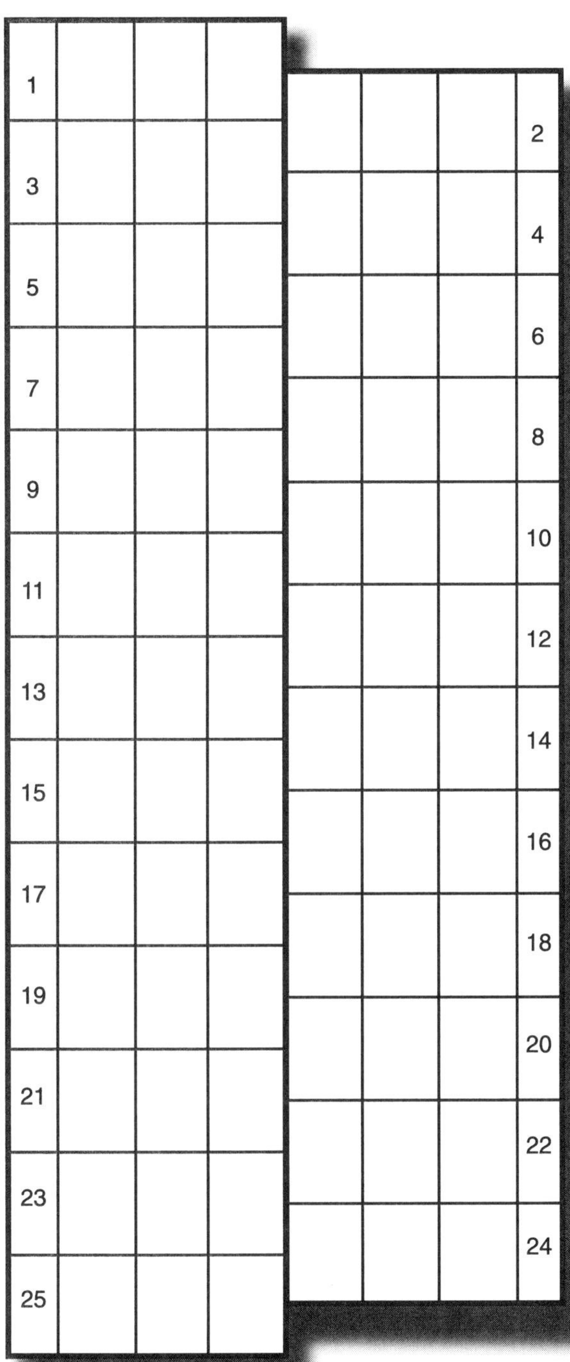

1-2. A male cat
2-3. Carefully planned to achieve a goal
3-4. Any tree bearing lemons, limes, oranges, etc.
4-5. A person who rides the waves on a board
5-6. Fits, prepares, or equips for use again
6-7. Steps for getting over a fence
7-8. Rarely; not often
8-9. An independent unit that forms part of a larger structure
9-10. Escapes by quickness or cleverness
10-11. Automobiles with front and back seats
11-12. Traps small animals with a noose
12-13. A public message preached by a minister
13-14. Unowned land between enemies
14-15. Small mollusks that crawl very slowly
15-16. Splinter; long, thin piece of wood
16-17. Call bad names; abuse with words
17-18. Arrive at truth by questioning or logic
18-19. A game using X's and O's, ___-___-toe
19-20. A plant that cats like
20-21. Claw of a lobster used to grip or pinch
21-22. Put music, words, or sounds on a tape
22-23. Hangs down; bends down
23-24. Becomes bad or unfit for use; damages
24-25. Glides over a smooth surface

Name: ____________________ Date: ____________

Back and Forth Puzzle: *Unusual Vocabulary Challenge #7*

Directions: Read the clues carefully and print your answer in the appropriate boxes. The last three letters of answer #1 become the first three letters of answer #2 and so on. (All of the even-numbered answers read from right to left.)

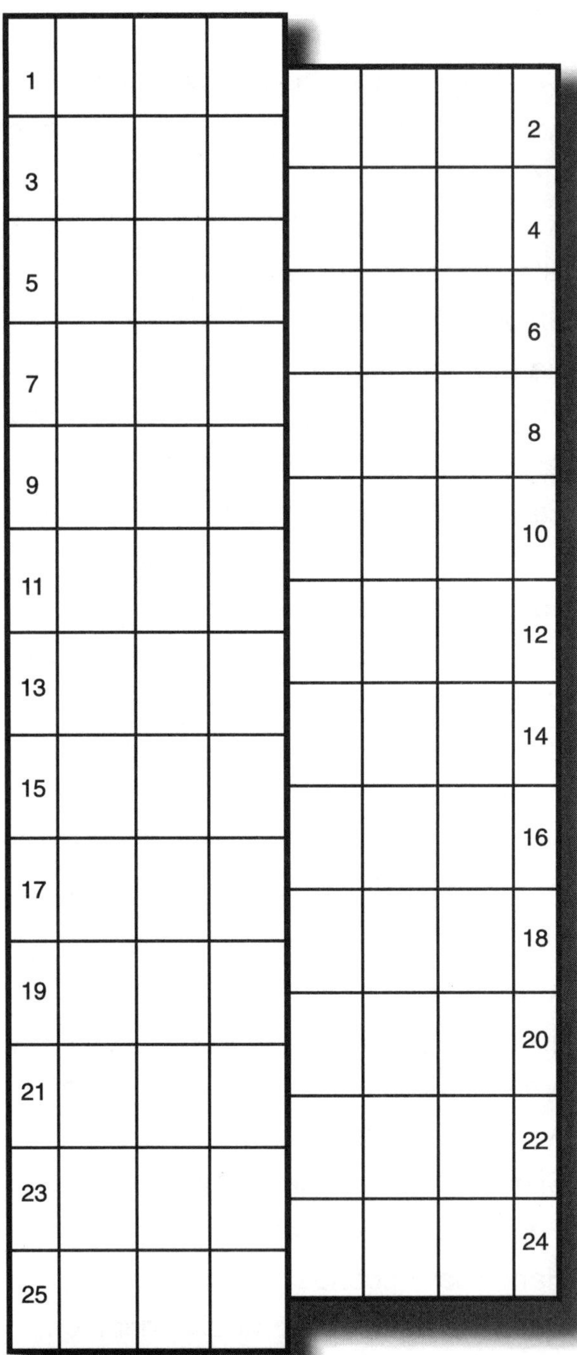

1-2. Something that hops
2-3. Forces back; drives away; drives back
3-4. Rests the body and the mind
4-5. Poured out (curses); vomited
5-6. Loose skin hanging from the neck of a cow
6-7. Lack of color from fear or illness; paleness
7-8. Moved by turning over and over
8-9. Searches carefully for information
9-10. The plural of one more than six
10-11. Moves in a stealthy, sly way
11-12. Glided or moved along on skates
12-13. A small item or particular part
13-14. Responsible; bound by law to pay
14-15. Joints between the upper arms and forearms
15-16. Faints
16-17. Goes about in a sneaking, prying way
17-18. Utensils with a shallow bowl and a handle
18-19. Breathed during sleep with a harsh sound
19-20. Make fun of; laugh at in scorn
20-21. Prepared for publication (corrected errors)
21-22. Hold back; delay; hold as a prisoner
22-23. A vitamin
23-24. Most pleasing; most agreeable
24-25. An African fly

Name: ______________________________ Date: ________________

Back and Forth Puzzle: *Unusual Vocabulary Challenge #8*

Directions: Read the clues carefully and print your answer in the appropriate boxes. The last three letters of answer #1 become the first three letters of answer #2 and so on. (All of the even-numbered answers read from right to left.)

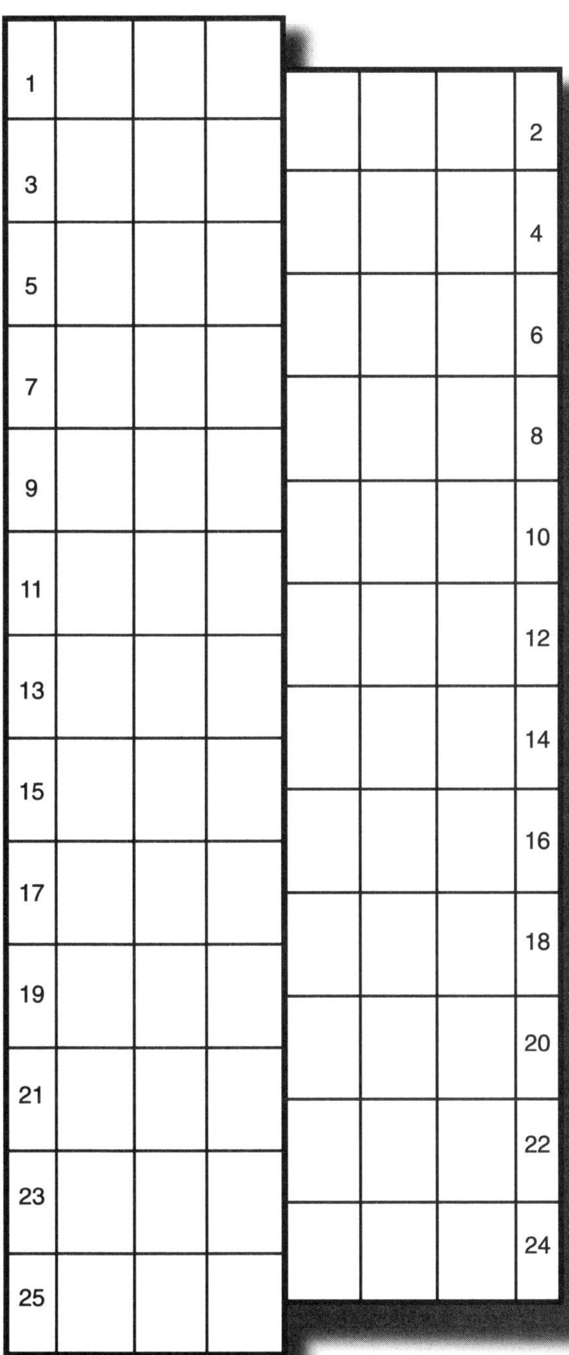

1-2. Splinter; a long, thin piece of wood
2-3. Go back; return
3-4. Entertains with food, drink, or amusement
4-5. One's social or professional standing
5-6. A person who followed an army and sold provisions
6-7. Something that is removed and laid again
7-8. A crown; something resembling a crown
8-9. The officers were decorated with many ____.
9-10. A person trading in slaves; a slave ship
10-11. Takes great pleasure; makes merry
11-12. Catnaps; dozes
12-13. Utters words with the voice
13-14. Glides over the ice with special boots
14-15. A breed of long-haired hunting dog
15-16. Delay the progress of; hinder; keep back
16-17. A box with handles that slides in and out of a desk
17-18. A money payment given or offered
18-19. Covered with cloth falling loosely in folds
19-20. Banish; exile; remove
20-21. Soldiers
21-22. Single cells that grow into new fungi
22-23. To have worked for; to have done one's duty
23-24. Completely without; empty
24-25. High-vacuum electron tubes

Name: ______________________________ Date: ________________

Acrostic Puzzle: *Antonyms #1*

Directions: Think of an antonym for each of the given words and write your answer in the numbered spaces. After you find an answer, transfer each numbered letter to the corresponding box in the grid. When you have completed the puzzle, you will know the answer to the following: What did the school nurse say to the student?

MARE	___ ___ ___ ___ ___ ___ ___ ___ (15 18 25 33 46 49 31 48)
PULL	___ ___ ___ ___ (36 21 11 34)
RENEW	___ ___ ___ ___ ___ ___ (42 45 13 5 43 47)
GLOOMY	___ ___ ___ ___ ___ ___ (16 37 41 50 9 19)
DISREGARDS	___ ___ ___ ___ ___ ___ ___ (10 40 32 14 35 20 29)
SOLO	*D* *U* *O* (24 12 6)
COUNTRY	___ ___ ___ ___ (39 27 22 26)
ME	___ ___ ___ (1 2 3)
THOUGHTLESSNESS	___ ___ ___ ___ ___ ___ ___ (52 30 23 7 8 51 28)
CHEAP	___ ___ ___ ___ (44 17 38 4)

1	2	3	4		5	6 *O*	7	8
9		10	11	12 *U*	13	14	15	
16	17	18	19	20	21		22	23
24 *D*	25	26		27	28		29	30
31	32	33	34		35		36	37
38	39	40	41	42	43	44		45
46	47		48	49	50	51	52	

Name: ______________________________ Date: ______________

Acrostic Puzzle: *Antonyms #2*

Directions: Think of an antonym for each of the given words and write your answer in the numbered spaces. After you find an answer, transfer each numbered letter to the corresponding box in the grid. When you have completed the puzzle, you will know the answer to the following: What was the student's complaint to the cafeteria worker?

STERN ___ ___ ___ ___ ___ ___ ___
20 12 55 53 49 32 1

FAIL ___ ___ ___ ___ ___ ___ ___ ___
16 51 10 15 33 7 28 35

HAPPINESS ___ ___ ___ ___ ___ ___
8 24 25 26 14 37

DECELERATE ___ ___ ___ ___ ___
6 9 44 3 11

BRAKE ___ ___ ___ ___
23 34 28 31

YOUTH old ___ ___ ___
21 48 42

DELICATE ___ ___ ___ ___ ___
2 45 13 29 38

INNER ___ ___ ___ ___ ___
36 40 50 47 4

NARROW ___ ___ ___ ___
41 30 22 5

TASTELESS ___ ___ ___ ___ ___ ___
18 54 46 39 43 27

BACKYARD front ___ ___ ___ ___
17 19 52 31

1	2	3	4	5	6		7		8
9	10	11	12	13		14	15		16
17		18	19	20	21	22		23	24
25	26	27		28		29	30	31	32
33		34	35	36	37		38	39	40
	41	42	43	44		45		46	47
48	49	50	51	52	53	54	55		

Name: ______________________________ Date: ____________________

Acrostic Puzzle: *Antonyms #3*

Directions: Think of an antonym for each of the given words and write your answer in the numbered spaces. After you find an answer, transfer each numbered letter to the corresponding box in the grid. When you have completed the puzzle, you will know the answer to the following: What did the old fisherman say to the young lad?

ERECTS ___ ___ ___ ___ ___
36 12 30 18 34

WEARY ___ ___ ___ ___ ___ ___ ___ ___ ___
10 51 20 40 45 27 15 9 3

ARID ___ ___ ___ ___ ___
17 33 29 28 24

FORGET ___ ___ ___ ___ ___
11 44 35 32 59

GOOD ___ ___ ___
56 57 1

SMOOTH ___ ___ ___ ___ ___ ___ ___ ___
42 36 2 53 13 50 45 1

SANE ___ ___ ___ ___ ___ ___ ___
47 3 26 33 49 37 58

MISERY ___ ___ ___ ___ ___ ___ ___
31 58 22 38 19 55 4

BORROWED ___ ___ ___ ___
50 14 53 49

HATE ___ ___ ___ ___
46 52 8 54

RETURNED ___ ___ ___ ___
48 41 5 13

PATHOS ___ ___ ___ ___ ___
39 6 17 16 10

FAT ___ ___ ___ ___
43 25 21 53

TOE ___ ___ ___ ___
23 7 12 3

1	2	3		4	5	6		7	8
9	10		11	12	13	14		15	16
17	18		19		20	21	22	23	
24	25	26	27		28	29	30	31	?
32	33		34	35	36		37		38
39	40	41	42		43	44	45		46
47	48	49	50	51		52	53	54	55
	56	57	58	59					

Name: ______________________________ Date: ____________________

Acrostic Puzzle: *Synonyms #1*

Directions: Think of a synonym for each of the given words and write your answer in the numbered spaces. After you find an answer, transfer each numbered letter to the corresponding box in the grid. When you have completed the puzzle, you will know the answer to the following: How do you know when a school is really haunted?

REBELLIOUS ___ ___ ___ ___ ___ ___ ___
31 11 33 14 37 28 50

ILL-NATURED ___ ___ ___ ___ ___
28 5 24 35 7

SNATCH ___ ___ ___ ___ ___ ___
4 13 9 29 40 41

COUCH ___ ___ ___ ___
17 21 15 16

SHAGGY ___ ___ ___ ___ ___
36 26 47 48 7

CHILLY ___ ___ ___ ___
18 42 43 13

LEAP ___ ___ ___
25 20 46

AN ISSUE ___ ___ ___ ___ ___ ___ ___
30 31 23 35 49 8 6

SULKY ___ ___ ___ ___ ___ ___
38 27 44 22 11 6

MELT ___ ___ ___ ___
10 19 5 3

CUNNING ___ ___ ___
39 12 7

PHANTOM ___ ___ ___ ___ ___ ___
45 46 34 48 32 29

WAIL ___ ___ ___ ___
1 2 3 22

1	2	3		4	5	6	
7	8	9		10	11	12	13
	14	15		16		17	18
19	20	21	22		23	24	
25	26	27	28	29	30	31	?
32	33		34	35		36	37
38		39	40	41	42	43	44
	45	46	47	48	49	50	

Name: ______________________ Date: ______________

Acrostic Puzzle: *Synonyms #2*

Directions: Think of a synonym for each of the given words and write your answer in the numbered spaces. After you find an answer, transfer each numbered letter to the corresponding box in the grid. When you have completed the puzzle, you will know the answer to the following: What snack do children enjoy at recess?

PREVENT ___ ___ ___ ___ ___ ___
2 47 38 10 41 35

PONDERED ___ ___ ___ ___ ___ ___ ___
1 29 13 34 28 22 39

SATISFY ___ ___ ___ ___ ___ ___
46 31 43 6 45 50

IDEA ___ ___ ___ ___ ___ ___
7 11 24 47 21 26

SULK ___ ___ ___ ___
30 25 37 20

SPOTLESS ___ ___ ___ ___ ___
49 16 41 32 38

WORSHIPPED ___ ___ ___ ___ ___ ___
23 8 36 40 22 14

STOPPED ___ ___ ___ ___ ___ ___
5 19 32 51 48 10

PUNTS ___ ___ ___ ___ ___
18 17 42 12 44

REMAIN ___ ___ ___ ___
15 20 3 9

HAMBURGER ___ ___ ___ ___ ___
30 6 4 27 33

1	2	3	4		5	6	7	8
9		10	11		12	13	14	15
	16	17	18	19		20	21	
22	23	24		25	26		27	28
29		30	31	32	33	34	35	36
37	38	39	?	40	41	42	43	44
45		46	47	48	49	50	51	

Name: ______________________________ Date: ____________________

Acrostic Puzzle: *Synonyms #3*

Directions: Think of a synonym for each of the given words and write your answer in the numbered spaces. After you find an answer, transfer each numbered letter to the corresponding box in the grid. When you have completed the puzzle, you will know the answer to the following: Why do some students simply not come to school?

DAZED ___ ___ ___ ___ ___ ___ ___ ___ ___ ___
41 36 1 11 33 51 18 38 43 49

TERMS ___ ___ ___ ___ ___ ___ ___ ___ ___ ___
29 31 48 12 47 45 11 5 44 13

SNARLED ___ ___ ___ ___ ___ ___ ___
17 16 32 1 33 9 4

BANQUET ___ ___ ___ ___ ___
14 25 40 6 19

FABLES ___ ___ ___ ___ ___
46 37 45 30 42

DECAY ___ ___ ___
16 27 34

STRANGLE ___ ___ ___ ___ ___
22 2 7 10 50

SAYING ___ ___ ___ ___ ___
24 15 26 20 23

BASHFUL ___ ___ ___
28 35 3

RESIDENCE ___ ___ ___ ___
30 21 8 39

1	2	3		4	5		6	7
8	9		10	11	12	13		14
15	16	17	18	19		20	21	
22	23	24	25		26	27		28
39	30	31	32	33	?	34	35	36
37	38	39		40	41	42	43	44
45	-	46	47	48	49	50	51	

Name: ______________________ Date: ______________

Split the Diamond Puzzle: *Scrambled Words #1*

Directions: Unscramble each word. The first and last two answers (the boldfaced letters) are given. When finished, follow the shaded boxes to reveal a message. Copy the message out on the lines below.

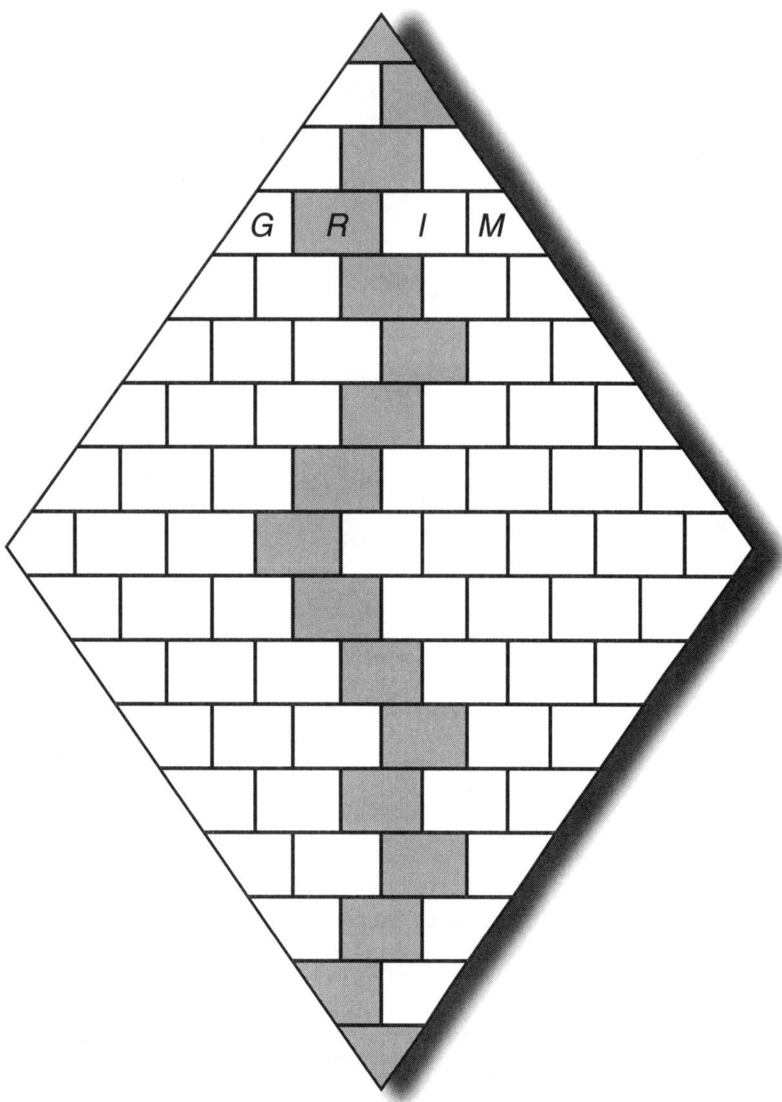

Y
T O
G U B
M G I R
T T R A E
S E A M D R
G G G I N O J
G N I O O P S W
O O P P E N N T S
E N T O B E D I
L E S M E D D
I N D D E E
S I P K C
R O T T
E A D
E T
R

___ ___ ___ R ___ ___ ___ ___ ___ ___ ___ ___ ___ ___ ___ ___ ___ ___ ___.

Name: ______________________________ Date: ______________

Split the Diamond Puzzle: *Scrambled Words #2*

Directions: Unscramble each word. The first and last two answers (the boldfaced letters) are given. When finished, follow the shaded boxes to reveal a message. Copy the message out on the lines below.

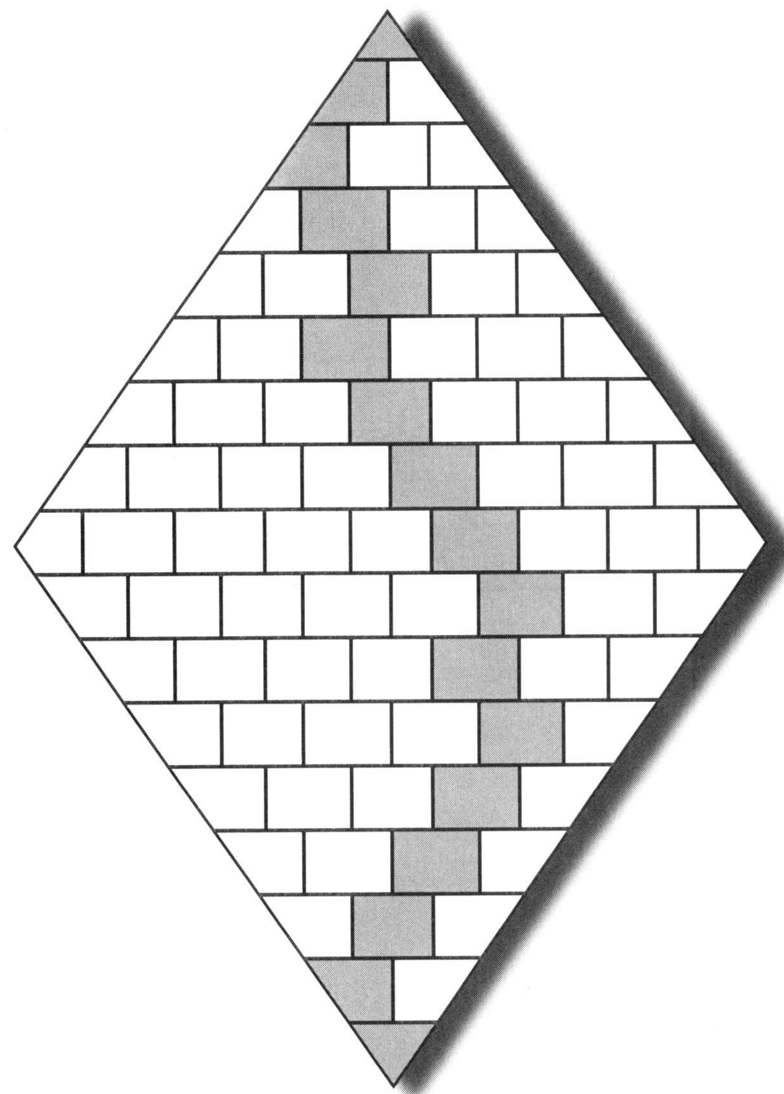

I

M E

A C S

C U D K

I N C S A

C A I N S E

R E A L C E S

C I S S S S O R

H O L U P S T E R

F U L T C H W A

N U S N R U B

A C C K L E

O C A C A

S G B A

A R N

I N

N

__ __ __ __ __ __ __ __ __ __ __ __ __ __ __ __ __ __ __ __ __ __ __.

Name: ______________________________ Date: ________________

Split the Diamond Puzzle: *Scrambled Words #3*

Directions: Unscramble each word. The first and last two answers (the boldfaced letters) are given. When finished, follow the shaded boxes to reveal a message. Copy the message out on the lines below.

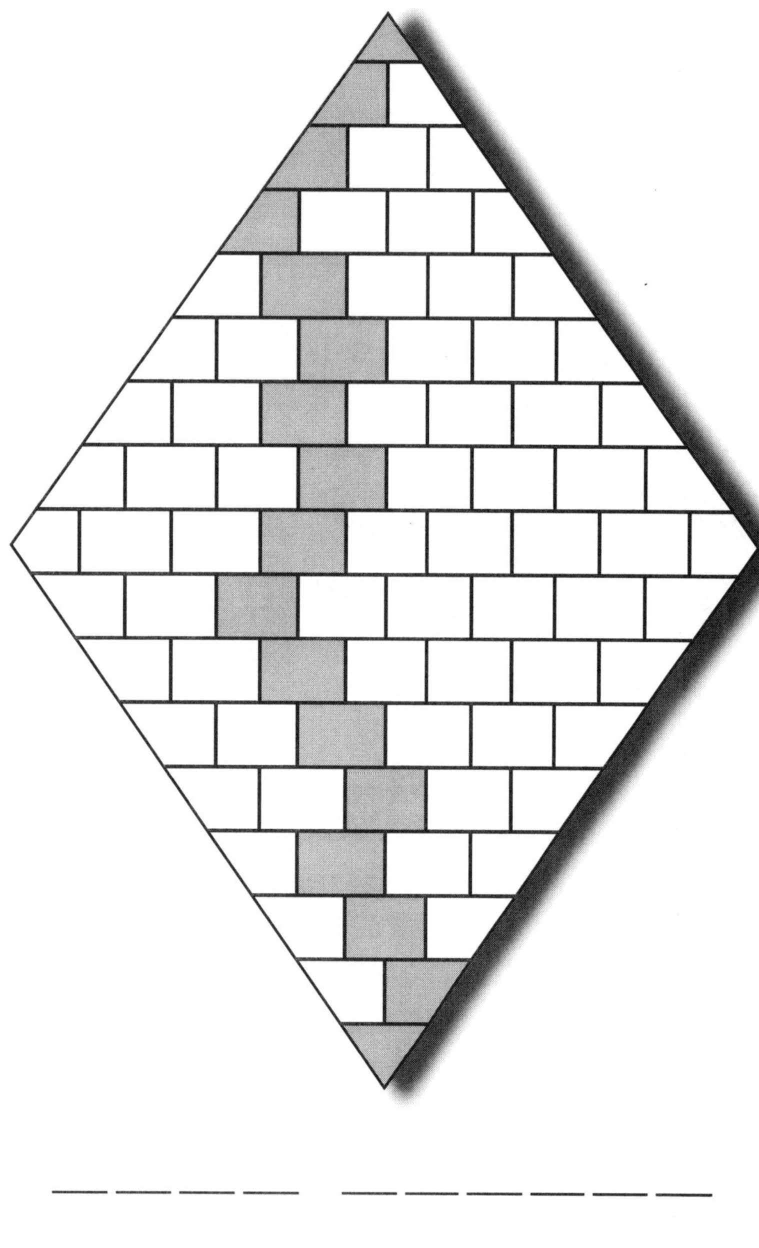

W

O R

A G R

L T K I

D R H Y O

K S B R C I

E A T H E R B

P O X L A L M S

D R O P U C G N I

T E D O R S A S

S S A E D U M

M U L C S Y

K S O C R

H E C A

D N E

A S

S

_ _ _ _ _ _ _ _ _ _ _ _ _ _

_ _ _ _ _ _ _ _ _ _ _ _ _ _.

Name: ______________________ Date: ______________

Split the Diamond Puzzle: *Scrambled Words #4*

Directions: Unscramble each word. The first and last two answers (the boldfaced letters) are given. When finished, follow the shaded boxes to reveal a message. Copy the message out on the lines below.

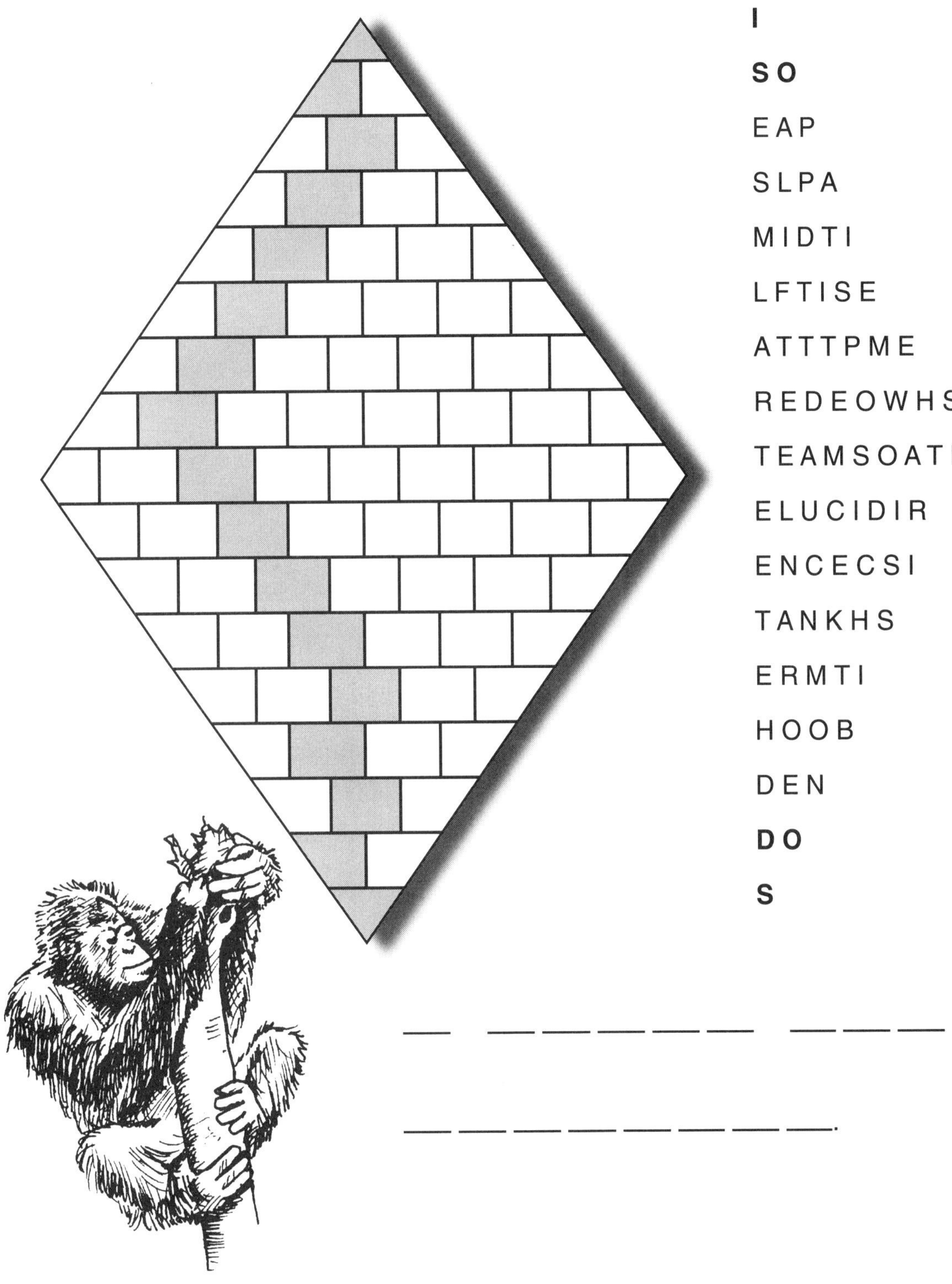

I

S O

E A P

S L P A

M I D T I

L F T I S E

A T T T P M E

R E D E O W H S

T E A M S O A T B

E L U C I D I R

E N C E C S I

T A N K H S

E R M T I

H O O B

D E N

D O

S

__ __ __ __ __ __ __ __ __ __ __ __

__ __ __ __ __ __ __ __ __.

Name: ______________________________ Date: ______________

Word Game: *Vocabulary With "TH'"Combinations*

Directions: The 25 words below all contain the letters "TH" in some combination. Read the clues carefully and complete each word in the puzzle.

T	H			
T	H			
T	H			
T	H			
T	H			
T	H	*O*	*R*	*N*
T	H			
T	H			
	T	H		
	T	H		
		T	H	
		T	H	
		T	H	
		T	H	
		T	H	
			T	H
			T	H
			T	H
			T	H
			T	H
T				H
T				H
T				H
T				H
T				H

1. beat rapidly; strongly
2. opposite of here
3. pound; thud; hammer
4. use your head
5. main idea; subject; topic
6. prickle on a plant
7. part of the leg between the hip and knee
8. dense; set close together
9. clear sky; regions high above us
10. remaining; additional or further
11. narrow walkways
12. winged insects flying mostly at night
13. apply water to; get clean
14. to give a tenth
15. a machine that holds and shapes wood
16. one-twelfth of a year
17. the ending of life in humans and animals
18. opening through which food passes
19. moor; open wasteland with low bushes
20. one of the planets
21. one of the hard, bone-like parts in the mouth
22. place part of the body against and feel
23. not a lie
24. rubbish
25. you have 32 of them

Name: ______________________________ Date: ____________________

Word Game: *Vocabulary With "EN" Combinations*

Directions: The 25 words below all contain the letters "EN" in some combination. Read the clues carefully and complete each word in the puzzle.

E	N			
E	N			
E	N			
E	N			
E	N			
	E	N		
	E	N		
	E	N		
	E	N		
	E	N		
		E	N	
		E	N	
		E	N	
		E	N	
		E	N	
			E	N
			E	N
			E	N
			E	N
			E	N
	E			N
	E			N
	E			N
	E			N
	E			N

1. come after; follow; happen as a result
2. give money or property; furnish with a gift
3. to be happy with
4. a messenger; a diplomat
5. a hostile force, nation, group, or person; a foe
6. stretched tight; showing strain; edgy
7. something put around a yard
8. a prefix meaning hundredth (1/100)
9. the poison of snakes and spiders
10. thick; closely packed together
11. small brown or gray songbirds
12. to pay out money; use up time
13. a person or company that acts for another
14. a smell; the sense of smell
15. to mix together; shade into each other
16. frequently; many times
17. adult females
18. make or become lively
19. past participle of *rise*
20. poplar tree whose leaves rustle in breezes
21. the period of power of a ruler
22. a car seating four or more people
23. condescend; think fit
24. initiate; another word for start
25. a lucky number; Roman numeral VII

Name: ________________________________ Date: ____________________

Word Game: *Vocabulary With "SP" Combinations*

Directions: The 25 words below all contain the letters "SP" in some combination. Read the clues carefully and complete each word in the puzzle.

S	P				1. pay out money for purchases
S	P				2. revenge; ill will
S	P				3. quickness; haste; swiftness
S	P				4. games involving skill and physical exertion
S	P				5. the region outside the earth's atmosphere
S			P		6. stores or buildings where materials are sold
S			P		7. outward look of a person's body
S			P		8. where people go skiing
S			P		9. cuts with scissors; short snappy action
S			P		10. a flight of stairs
S		P			11. leaflike division of the calyx of a flower
S		P			12. full of sap; juicy
S		P			13. appetizing; mouth-watering
S		P			14. soaking wet; foolish; sentimental
S		P			15. of high quality; great work
			S	P	16. fastener on a bracelet
			S	P	17. to seize firmly with the hand
		S	P		18. flying insects that sting
		S	P		19. coarse files used to remove unevenness
S				P	20. small boat with one mast
S				P	21. having a sharp slope
S				P	22. wet, soft land; spongy land
S				P	23. a small part left over; a small piece
S				P	24. an edge that cuts easily
S				P	25. rest the body and mind

Name: ______________________________ Date: ________________

Word Game: *Vocabulary With "LE" Combinations*

Directions: The 25 words below all contain the letters "LE" in some combination. Read the clues carefully and complete each word in the puzzle.

L	E					1. fatal; causing death
L	E					2. narrow shelves at the base of windows
L	E					3. bars used for raising or moving something
L	E					4. a written message that is mailed
L	E					5. one who provides guidance or direction
	L	E				6. smart; bright; intelligent
	L	E				7. give enjoyment to; used for politeness
	L	E				8. tired
	L	E				9. part of a garment that covers the arms
	L	E				10. a solemn promise
		L	E			11. choose; pick out
		L	E			12. narrow strips of water; entrances
		L	E			13. assert without proof; assert or declare
		L	E			14. become more tender and merciful
		L	E			15. narrow back streets
				L	E	16. laugh in a silly or nervous way
				L	E	17. a struggle; argument; bother; annoy
				L	E	18. slender tool with sharp point used in sewing
				L	E	19. a pointed, hanging stick of ice
				L	E	20. a part of a thing made to be held
L					E	21. a group of teams following a schedule
L					E	22. a young girl; lass
L					E	23. number of lines of printed matter on a page
L					E	24. not big or large; small
L					E	25. find out the exact location of

Name: ______________________________ Date: ______________

Pair of Diamonds Puzzle Template

Directions: Read and answer each of the clues carefully. When finished, read down the left side of each diamond to reveal a hidden message.

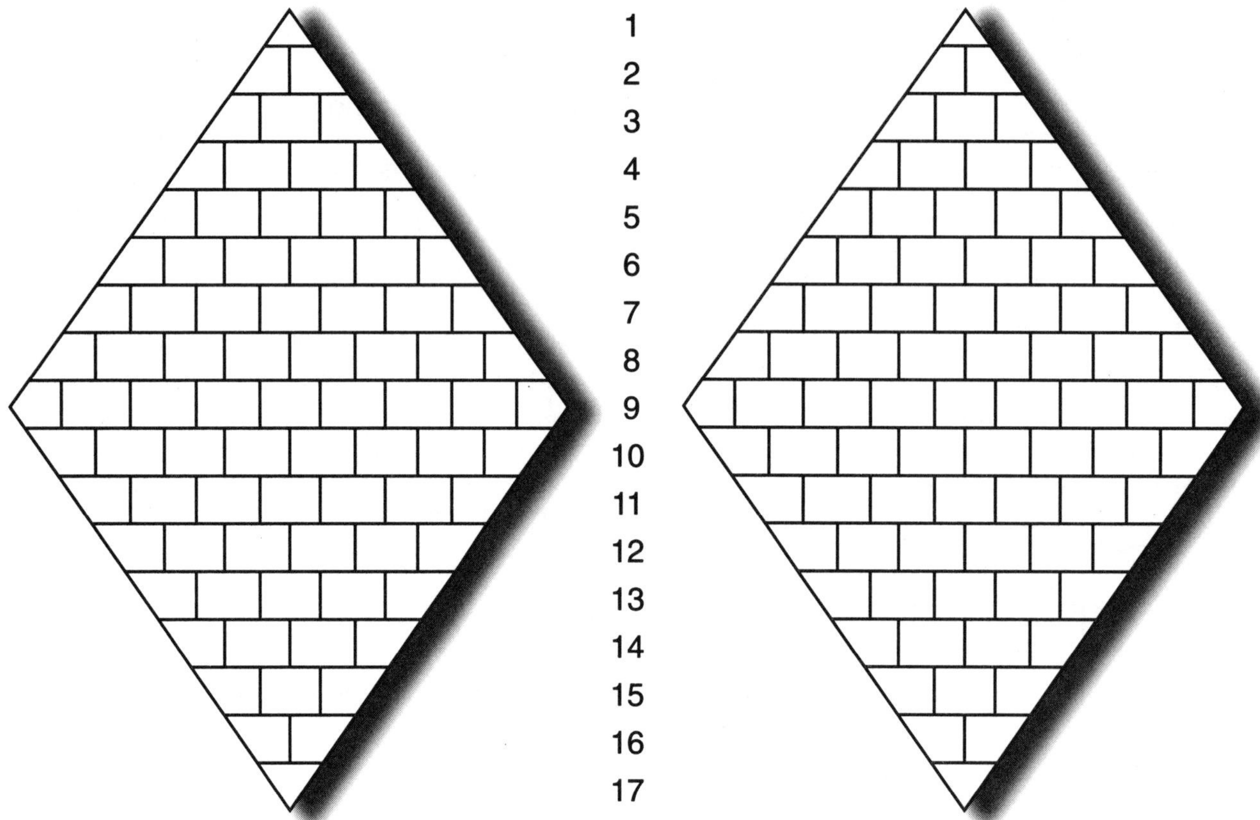

Name: ______________________________ Date: ____________________

Zig-Zag Topics Template

Directions: Answer the clues correctly. Take the letters in order from each of the shaded areas and a message will appear.

Name: ______________________________ Date: ________________

Back and Forth Puzzle Template

Directions: Read the clues carefully and print your answer in the appropriate boxes. The last three letters of answer #1 become the first three letters of answer #2 and so on. (All of the even-numbered answers read from right to left.)

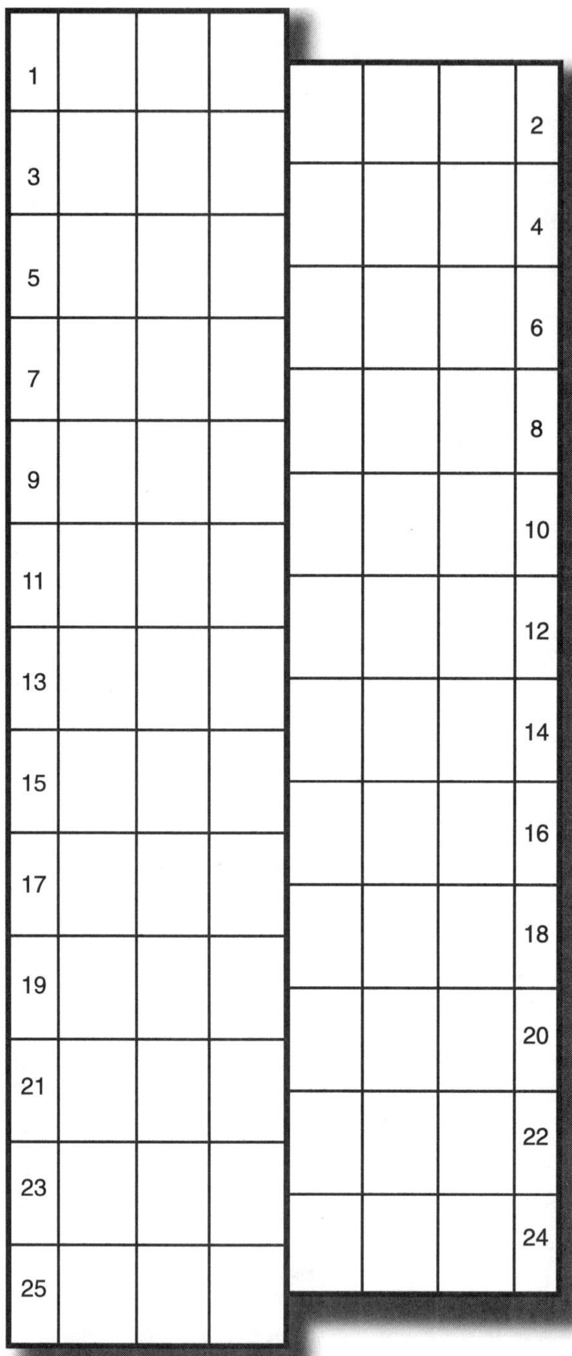

Name: ____ Date: ______________________

Split the Diamond Puzzle Template

Directions: Unscramble each word. The first and last two answers (the boldfaced letters) are given. When finished, follow the shaded boxes to reveal a message. Copy the message out on the lines below.

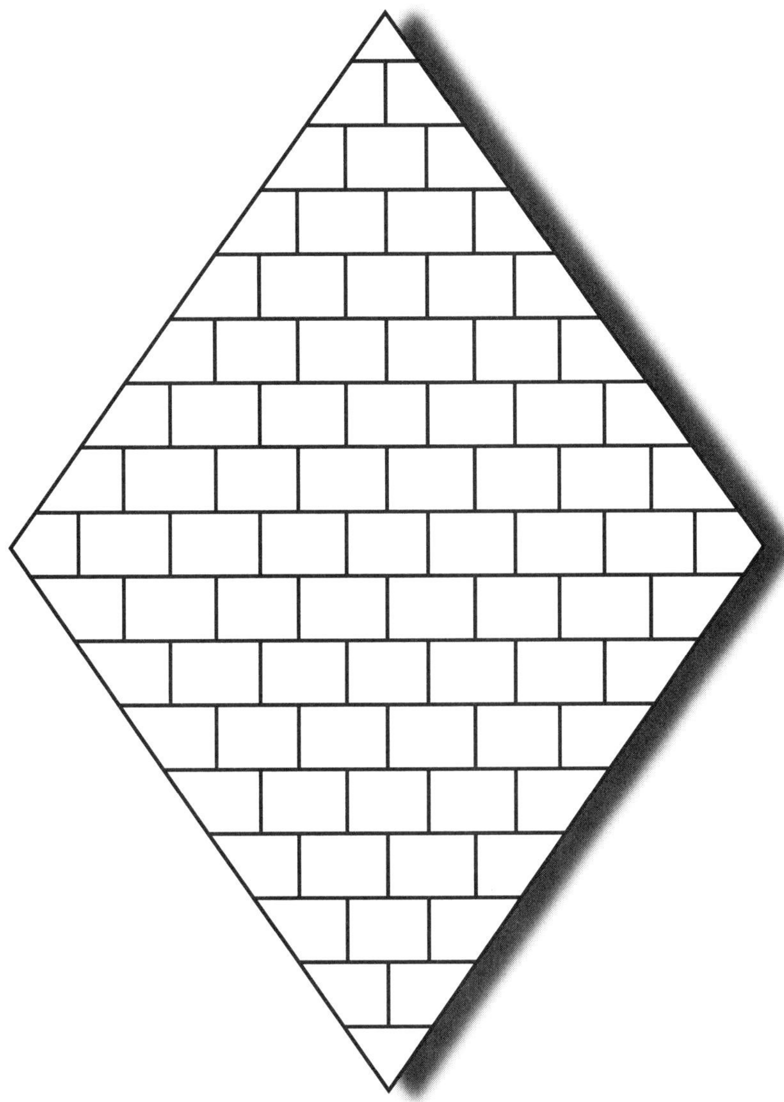

Answer Keys

Pair of Diamonds: Holiday Greetings (p. 4)
Left Diamond:
1. M
2. er
3. raw
4. rare
5. you're
6. cannot
7. holiday
8. relative
9. important
10. stallion
11. terrify
12. midget
13. actor
14. soar
15. ace
16. no
17. D

Right Diamond:
1. h
2. ad
3. pal
4. pear
5. youth
6. ninety
7. evident
8. weddings
9. yesterday
10. engineer
11. African
12. refuse
13. teach
14. oath
15. ads
16. la
17. L

Message: Merry Christmas and Happy New Year to all.

Pair of Diamonds: Lunch Specials (p. 5)
Left Diamond:
1. p
2. I'd
3. zoo
4. zero
5. after
6. afraid
7. newborn
8. downpour
9. hothouses
10. operetta
11. tighten
12. drakes
13. omits
14. grin
15. day
16. ac
17. y

Right Diamond:
1. s
2. am
3. ran
4. east
5. altos
6. thorny
7. rebuild
8. eighteen
9. amazement
10. theyhave
11. friends
12. orient
13. ready
14. king
15. ill
16. dr
17. s

Message: Pizza and hot dog days are a treat for kids.

Pair of Diamonds: Best Friends (p. 6)
Left Diamond:
1. e
2. at
3. rip
4. lung
5. young
6. icicle
7. natural
8. Thursday
9. hamburger
10. elevates
11. scalene
12. chilly
13. heard
14. once
15. Oct
16. ly
17. y

Right Diamond:
1. e
2. as
3. rid
4. four
5. razor
6. infant
7. enlarge
8. nickname
9. difficult
10. secondly
11. article
12. return
13. enjoy
14. melt
15. are
16. do
17. e

Message: Early in the school year friends are made.

Pair of Diamonds: Witches and Goblins (p. 7)
Left Diamond:
1. a
2. la
3. lad
4. cost
5. heart
6. invert
7. ladybug
8. duckling
9. racetrack
10. eastward
11. narrate
12. tailor
13. ranch
14. idea
15. cab
16. kg
17. o

Right Diamond:
1. r
2. ti
3. rag
4. echo
5. acorn
6. talent
7. octopus
8. nicotine
9. hobgoblin
10. anaconda
11. leotard
12. litter
13. opera
14. wolf
15. end
16. ed
17. n

Message: All children trick or treat on Halloween.

Answer Keys

Pair of Diamonds: March Madness (p. 8)
Left Diamond:
1. t
2. ha
3. ewe
4. menu
5. ankle
6. recent
7. cricket
8. harpoons
9. buccaneer
10. reforest
11. embrace
12. answer
13. knead
14. iron
15. sin
16. ad
17. t

Right Diamond:
1. I
2. MD
3. emu
4. toil
5. onion
6. reduce
7. extinct
8. landlord
9. abandoned
10. xmastime
11. achieve
12. nitwit
13. dirty
14. pony
15. lag
16. am
17. y

Message: The March break is a time to relax and play.

Pair of Diamonds: Summer Fun (p. 9)
Left Diamond:
1. b
2. aa
3. sad
4. exit
5. black
6. asthma
7. lobster
8. lollipop
9. assistant
10. November
11. dentist
12. stench
13. ocean
14. calm
15. car
16. er
17. r

Right Diamond:
1. a
2. rd
3. eve
4. mild
5. you're
6. Sahara
7. unsound
8. memorize
9. milkshake
10. elephant
11. rapidly
12. scream
13. parka
14. okay
15. ram
16. to
17. s

Message: Baseball and soccer are my summer sports.

Pair of Diamonds: Two Hundred Days of the Year (p. 10)
Left Diamond:
1. e
2. vc
3. etc
4. read
5. yours
6. scurry
7. pasture
8. entirely
9. cranberry
10. immature
11. antique
12. length
13. denim
14. area
15. yam
16. cd
17. R

Right Diamond:
1. e
2. ad
3. tan
4. evil
5. scuba
6. second
7. couldn't
8. hexagons
9. orchestra
10. overheat
11. luggage
12. seesaw
13. paddy
14. iron
15. red
16. i'd
17. t

Message: Every special day creates school spirit.

Pair of Diamonds: Cupid's Special Day (p. 11)
Left Diamond:
1. o
2. no
3. vim
4. ants
5. lanky
6. effort
7. nothing
8. talented
9. interview
10. November
11. elevate
12. summit
13. depth
14. amen
15. yew
16. wk
17. e

Right Diamond:
1. a
2. la
3. let
4. gave
5. igloo
6. velvet
7. equator
8. magician
9. orangutan
10. magazine
11. finally
12. liquid
13. oasis
14. won't
15. ewe
16. Ra
17. s

Message: On Valentine's Day we all give Mom flowers.

Answer Keys

Combination Puzzle: Analogous Relationships #1 (p. 12)

1. minute
2. severe
3. expert
4. lessen
5. gather
6. jungle
7. polite
8. devout
9. saddle
10. horrid
11. blared
12. hammer

Combination Puzzle: Analogous Relationships #2 (p. 13)

1. circus
2. simple
3. impact
4. column
5. quiver
6. genius
7. affirm
8. guitar
9. eyelid
10. extend
11. pebble
12. sudden

Combination Puzzle: Analogous Relationships #3 (p. 14)

1. reward
2. advice
3. twenty
4. wizard
5. master
6. handle
7. recent
8. quarry
9. forest
10. drowse
11. camera
12. falter

Combination Puzzle: Analogous Relationships #4 (p. 15)

1. weight
2. bidder
3. wicked
4. liquid
5. bleach
6. divide
7. stable
8. beaded
9. clumsy
10. retort
11. ladder
12. stuffs

Combination Puzzle: Analogous Relationships #5 (p. 16)

1. remote
2. battle
3. barrel
4. thawed
5. artist
6. horror
7. canyon
8. letter
9. filter
10. kennel
11. fasten
12. absorb

Combination Puzzle: Analogous Relationships #6 (p. 17)

1. decade
2. quiver
3. delays
4. cement
5. hammer
6. radios
7. signal
8. single
9. melted
10. finger
11. ignore
12. stable

Combination Puzzle: Analogous Relationships #7 (p. 18)

1. costly
2. garnet
3. senior
4. defend
5. rubies
6. string
7. island
8. gather
9. design
10. judged
11. pepper
12. simmer

Combination Puzzle: Analogous Relationships #8 (p. 19)

1. gallop
2. manual
3. gleams
4. avenue
5. donkey
6. daring
7. admire
8. raisin
9. guitar
10. flames
11. folder
12. silent

Clues Galore: Build Your Vocabulary #1 (p. 20)

A. fur
roar
buds
fraud
SURFBOARD

B. siren
diet
stern
dines
RESIDENTS

C. chap
chart
crate
hut
PARACHUTE

Clues Galore: Build Your Vocabulary #2 (p. 21)

A. crone
pipe
pounce
ripe
PORCUPINE

B. rate
rope
train
note
OPERATION

C. serve
virus
ruse
pier
SUPERVISE

Clues Galore: Build Your Vocabulary #3 (p. 22)

A. flow
swore
fun
fuse
SUNFLOWER

B. rim
prime
teem
meet
PERIMETER

C. grasp
gene
sag
rage
PASSENGER

Clues Galore: Build Your Vocabulary #4 (p. 23)

A. male
mess
she
slam
SHAMELESS

B. burnt
tube
lure
true
TURBULENT

Answer Keys

C. new
pint
wove
pine
VIEWPOINT

Clues Galore: Build Your Vocabulary #5 (p. 24)

A. yes
trade
yeast
red
YESTERDAY

B. lair
real
pain
crop
PORCELAIN

C. hope
deep
head
pen
HEADPHONE

Clues Galore: Build Your Vocabulary #6 (p. 25)

A. less
real
close
class
CASSEROLE

B. rule
nose
lose
scene
ENCLOSURE

C. brow
near
brown
drake
BREAKDOWN

Zig-Zag Topics: Vocabulary Building #1 (p. 26)

1. steep
2. nouns
3. melon
4. valve
5. okapi
6. stink
7. sugar
8. empty
9. acute
10. steak
11. usher
12. elope
13. tapir
14. visio
15. knobs
16. holly
17. pedal
18. maybe
19. ashes
20. guide
21. pause
22. throb
23. field
24. Asian
25. aster
26. sweep

Message: Solving math problems is bliss.

Zig-Zag Topics: Vocabulary Building #2 (p. 27)

1. reply
2. seven
3. shawl
4. grade
5. cacti
6. stung
7. soggy
8. width
9. scent
10. kayak
11. hasn't
12. focus
13. syrup
14. spice
15. yours
16. sober
17. pearl
18. Xerox
19. spine
20. steal
21. shark
22. plexi
23. tried
24. singe
25. scene
26. excel

Message: Reading is a superb experience.

Zig-Zag Topics: Vocabulary Building #3 (p. 28)

1. rhyme
2. repel
3. bacon
4. sheen
5. lofts
6. first
7. trick
8. asset
9. adult
10. stiff
11. moist
12. roomy
13. purse
14. pleat
15. bloom
16. lemon
17. ready
18. error
19. stool
20. offer
21. third
22. Hindi
23. fried
24. Santa
25. adieu
26. saint

Message: Recess is a time to meet friends.

Zig-Zag Topics: Vocabulary Building #4 (p. 29)

1. stove
2. super
3. caper
4. valet
5. baker
6. combs
7. signs
8. satin
9. misty
10. teeth
11. resin
12. nasal
13. molar
14. niece
15. manly
16. enemy
17. vague
18. reign
19. ankle
20. alert
21. cards
22. cacti
23. paint
24. pagan
25. syrup
26. money

Message: Superb games are learned in gym.

Zig-Zag Topics: Scrambled Words #1 (p. 30)

1. eaten
2. exile
3. green
4. stern
5. panic
6. timid
7. mason
8. heart
9. igloo
10. aspen
11. piggy
12. share
13. place
14. pizza
15. misty
16. offer
17. toast
18. range
19. stamp
20. other
21. racer
22. ranch
23. refer
24. roast
25. group
26. table

Message: Exercise is great for the heart.

Zig-Zag Topics: Scrambled Words #2 (p. 31)

1. agony
2. apron
3. force
4. often
5. stump
6. trial
7. forth
8. relax
9. drawn
10. opens
11. prune
12. drape
13. fungi
14. broil
15. jelly
16. dream
17. badly
18. rapid
19. angle
20. music
21. novel
22. media
23. moist
24. olive
25. pilot
26. yearn

Message: A prepared pupil learns easily.

Last Letter-First Letter Puzzle: Animals Galore (p. 32)

1. robin
2. narwhal
3. lobster
4. ram
5. moose
6. elephant
7. toad
8. donkey
9. yak
10. kangaroo
11. ostrich
12. hyena
13. aardvark

Answer Keys

14. koala
15. armadillo
16. octopus
17. squirrel
18. lizard
19. deer

RAPTOR

Last Letter-First Letter Puzzle:
Law Enforcement (p. 33)

1. detectives
2. snoop
3. protect
4. testify
5. youngster
6. rookie
7. emergencies
8. sober
9. ruthless
10. scream
11. Mountie
12. experienced
13. disturb
14. bloodstains

VEST and GLASS

Last Letter-First Letter Puzzle:
Clothing and Accessories (p. 34)

1. jacket
2. trousers
3. shirt
4. tie
5. earring
6. gown
7. necklace
8. earmuffs
9. suit
10. turban
11. nightshirt
12. taste
13. eyeglasses
14. sandal
15. leotard
16. dress
17. scarf
18. feather

STRAIT

Last Letter-First Letter Puzzle:
Anyone Hungry? (p. 35)

1. potatoes
2. steak
3. ketchup
4. parsnip
5. plum
6. melon
7. nectarine
8. eel
9. lemongrass
10. squash
11. honeydew
12. walnut
13. turnip
14. pepper
15. radish
16. hash
17. honey
18. yams
19. salads

ROAST

Last Letter-First Letter Puzzle:
Vocabulary Development #1 (p. 36)

1. fussy
2. year
3. rhinoceros
4. September
5. reopen
6. numerator
7. ranch
8. happiness
9. stomp
10. pond
11. deck
12. key
13. yard
14. draft
15. tree
16. eleven
17. nip
18. panic
19. curl
20. limb
21. brow
22. wand
23. dam

PELICAN

Last Letter-First Letter Puzzle:
Vocabulary Development #2 (p. 37)

1. buffalo
2. oven
3. nasty
4. yodel
5. lumber
6. ruffle
7. eject
8. tarantula
9. adored
10. dew
11. witch
12. heroism
13. mop
14. pizza
15. askew
16. weld
17. dream
18. mess
19. strip
20. pickle
21. ear
22. ribbon
23. neigh

MANDOLIN

Last Letter-First Letter Puzzle:
Scrambled Words #1 (p. 38)

1. blast
2. tattoo
3. ocean
4. neck
5. kelp
6. penny
7. yeast
8. toxin
9. nickel
10. lobster
11. rough
12. hives
13. slump
14. prism
15. milk
16. knelt
17. trout
18. temple
19. evil
20. leap
21. pharaoh
22. herd
23. dab
24. battle

COCONUT

Last Letter-First Letter Puzzle:
Scrambled Words #2 (p. 39)

1. lion
2. nimble
3. enemy
4. yacht
5. temper
6. rough
7. horse
8. equip
9. pound
10. dream
11. mystery
12. youth
13. historic
14. castle
15. eyeball
16. lullaby
17. yogurt
18. tomb
19. burro
20. outcast
21. toes

BRAILLE

Reveal a Palindrome:
Missing Links #1 (p. 40)

moped	loose
steak	posts
fists	probe
botch	piper
greed	range
honey	watch

Message: Step on no pets.

Answer Keys

Reveal a Palindrome: Missing Links #2 (p. 41)

align, arson, bucks, claim, cower, drank, extol, glass, gross, heard, large, march, sassy, spank, stile, tawny, title, track, wicks

Message: Was it a car or a cat I saw?

Reveal a Palindrome: Missing Links #3 (p. 42)

bland, brash, chase, cones, flake, flame, jelly, knave, limbo, malls, nanny, nymph, opals, prawn, rents, reply, sandy, sects, tapes, trash, wrath

Message: A man, a plan, a canal—Panama.

Reveal a Palindrome: Missing Links #4 (p. 43)

arena, chive, cones, Crete, delta, denim, diner, ditty, gripe, mamba, mince, music, nosey, pilot, pithy, quite, roach, samba, slaps, space, trash

Message: Ten animals I slam in a net.

Reveal a Palindrome: Missing Links #5 (p. 44)

align, banks, brawn, bumpy, cower, flesh, gross, grove, inner, manor, medal, modes, quite, Romeo, rower, shade, spate, stele, tines

Message: Now, Ned, I am a maiden won.

Reveal a Palindrome: Missing Links #6 (p. 45)

cease, cedar, craft, draft, elbow, fiber, litho, pares, peary, peony, ratio, rinse, scale, scone, sense, siren, sodas, spore, stone, terse, wrath

Message: A rod, not a bar: a baton, Dora.

Reveal a Palindrome: Missing Links #7 (p. 46)

bathe, bowel, crimp, crook, drive, easel, emery, flame, fleck, grind, gross, lathe, lower, males, miser, paste, pilot, titan, tithe, trick, whale

Message: Was it Eliot's toilet I saw?

Reveal a Palindrome: Missing Links #8 (p. 47)

aroma, chops, cones, fresh, grand, grave, large, manor, perky, power, remit, rhyme, scape, small, sowed, tempo, tryst

Message: Yawn a more Roman way.

Fewer Clues: Build Your Vocabulary More #1 (p. 48)

A. crane, sure, inn, INSURANCE
B. tale, metal, can't, CATTLEMAN
C. trust, rant, toast, ASTRONAUT

Fewer Clues: Build Your Vocabulary More #2 (p. 49)

A. shed, hone, ties, DISHONEST
B. gender, large, day, LEGENDARY
C. clue, line, coat, INOCULATE

Fewer Clues: Build Your Vocabulary More #3 (p. 50)

A. armed, lame, mad, MARMALADE
B. pity, rest, potter, POSTERITY
C. wade, vital, dial, TIDAL WAVE

Fewer Clues: Build Your Vocabulary More #4 (p. 51)

A. touch, cone, hunted, UNTOUCHED
B. vote, never, rule, VOLUNTEER
C. tassel, sale, late, TASTELESS

Fewer Clues: Build Your Vocabulary More #5 (p. 52)

A. vile, rate, save, RELATIVES
B. treat, rude, grit, GRATITUDE
C. misery, chime, city, CHEMISTRY

Answer Keys

Fewer Clues: Build Your Vocabulary More #6 (p. 53)

A. grade
rise
died
DISREGARD

B. potion
rope
rate
OPERATION

C. nipple
pipe
pale
PINEAPPLE

Four-Squared Puzzle: Vocabulary Enrichment #1 (p. 54)

1.	fried	2.	stiff
	north		crate
	arrow		drake
	grimy		petty
	doing		rhyme
3.	dread	4.	still
	stand		shout
	dream		hairy
	night		flips
	raven		gross

Message: Form great friendships.

Four-Squared Puzzle: Vocabulary Enrichment #2 (p. 55)

1.	easel	2.	groom
	adult		prune
	blunt		clock
	trace		Bible
	koala		tasty
3.	cream	4.	elope
	coast		swoon
	bleed		cliff
	skull		brass
	acorn		close

Message: Education makes me wise.

Four-Squared Puzzle: Vocabulary Enrichment #3 (p. 56)

1.	weary	2.	swing
	bison		lunar
	mason		visit
	trade		birch
	bingo		mimic
3.	elder	4.	occur
	shaft		amend
	enter		anger
	after		stood
	index		flood

Message: Wisdom is a gift from God.

Four-Squared Puzzle: Vocabulary Enrichment #4 (p. 57)

1.	algae	2.	throb
	bikes		creep
	timed		usher
	stuff		atlas
	bongo		rapid
3.	bride	4.	sniff
	alert		lunch
	match		valor
	asset		sixty
	eject		grass

Message: Aim for the best results.

Four-Squared Puzzle: Vocabulary Enrichment #5 (p. 58)

1.	murky	2.	audio
	waist		grate
	baker		needy
	kneel		omits
	float		ivory
3.	gruff	4.	owner
	buddy		crisp
	diary		offer
	learn		group
	reply		pagan

Message: Make time to read for fun.

Four-Squared Puzzle: Vocabulary Enrichment #6 (p. 59)

1.	scrub	2.	steam
	curly		onion
	licks		cycle
	finch		essay
	grape		stool
3.	paint	4.	herbs
	music		awake
	downy		gnome
	usual		guard
	elbow		shock

Message: Success comes with work.

Back and Forth Puzzle: Unusual Vocabulary Challenge #1 (p. 60)

1-2. morsel
2-3. lesser
3-4. resorb
4-5. broker
5-6. reknit
6-7. tinner
7-8. rennet
8-9. tennis
9-10. singer
10-11. regret
11-12. terret
12-13. terser
13-14. resort
14-15. trocar
15-16. raceme
16-17. emerge
17-18. egrets
18-19. steeve
19-20. evened
20-21. dented
21-22. detain
22-23. niacin
23-24. nicest
24-25. tsetse

Back and Forth Puzzle: Unusual Vocabulary Challenge #2 (p. 61)

1-2. troops
2-3. sports
3-4. stripe
4-5. epilog
5-6. golfed
6-7. defied
7-8. Deimos
8-9. somber
9-10. rebels
10-11. sleeps
11-12. spewed
12-13. dewlap
13-14. pallet
14-15. teller
15-16. relaid
16-17. diadem
17-18. median
18-19. nailed
19-20. deluxe
20-21. exudes
21-22. sedans
22-23. snares
23-24. server
24-25. revved

Back and Forth Puzzle: Unusual Vocabulary Challenge #3 (p. 62)

1-2. dapper
2-3. repair
3-4. riatas
4-5. satang
5-6. gnawed
6-7. dewlap
7-8. pallor
8-9. rolled
9-10. deltas
10-11. satrap
11-12. parrot
12-13. torpid
13-14. dipped
14-15. depart
15-16. trails
16-17. sliver
17-18. revels
18-19. sleeve
19-20. everts
20-21. stripe
21-22. epilog
22-23. golfed
23-24. defile
24-25. elicit

Answer Keys

Back and Forth Puzzle: Unusual Vocabulary Challenge #4 (p. 63)

1-2. simmer
2-3. remark
3-4. kraals
4-5. slaver
5-6. revert
6-7. treble
7-8. elbows
8-9. swoons
9-10. snored
10-11. derris
11-12. sirens
12-13. sneaks
13-14. skates
14-15. setter
15-16. retort
16-17. troops
17-18. spoons
18-19. snowed
19-20. dewlap
20-21. pallet
21-22. teller
22-23. relics
23-24. scions
24-25. snoops

Back and Forth Puzzle: Unusual Vocabulary Challenge #5 (p. 64)

1-2. remark
2-3. krater
3-4. retort
4-5. troops
5-6. spoken
6-7. nekton
7-8. notion
8-9. noises
9-10. sestet
10-11. tetrad
11-12. darned
12-13. dental
13-14. latter
14-15. retina
15-16. animal
16-17. lamest
17-18. tsetse
18-19. esteem
19-20. meeker
20-21. reknit
21-22. tinder
22-23. redder
23-24. red ink
24-25. knight

Back and Forth Puzzle: Unusual Vocabulary Challenge #6 (p. 65)

1-2. tomcat
2-3. tactic
3-4. citrus
4-5. surfer
5-6. refits
6-7. stiles
7-8. seldom
8-9. module
9-10. eludes
10-11. sedans
11-12. snares
12-13. sermon
13-14. no man's
14-15. snails
15-16. sliver
16-17. revile
17-18. elicit
18-19. tic tac
19-20. catnip
20-21. pincer
21-22. record
22-23. droops
23-24. spoils
24-25. slides

Back and Forth Puzzle: Unusual Vocabulary Challenge #7 (p. 66)

1-2. hopper
2-3. repels
3-4. sleeps
4-5. spewed
5-6. dewlap
6-7. pallor
7-8. rolled
8-9. delves
9-10. sevens
10-11. sneaks
11-12. skated
12-13. detail
13-14. liable
14-15. elbows
15-16. swoons
16-17. snoops
17-18. spoons
18-19. snored
19-20. deride
20-21. edited
21-22. detain
22-23. niacin
23-24. nicest
24-25. tsetse

Back and Forth Puzzle: Unusual Vocabulary Challenge #8 (p. 67)

1-2. sliver
2-3. revert
3-4. treats
4-5. status
5-6. sutler
6-7. relaid
7-8. diadem
8-9. medals
9-10. slaver
10-11. revels
11-12. sleeps
12-13. speaks
13-14. skates
14-15. setter
15-16. retard
16-17. drawer
17-18. reward
18-19. draped
19-20. deport
20-21. troops
21-22. spores
22-23. served
23-24. devoid
24-25. diodes

Acrostic Puzzle: Antonyms #1 (p. 68)

Stallion Prod
Cancel Bright
Studies Duo
City You
Thought Dear

Message: Your cough sounds better today; it should, I practiced all night.

Acrostic Puzzle: Antonyms #2 (p. 69)

Lenient Hardy
Maintain Outer
Sorrow Wide
Speed Savory
Skid Yard
Age

Message: There's a spider on my salad. Sorry, I didn't know you were a vegetarian.

Acrostic Puzzle: Antonyms #3 (p. 70)

Razes Ecstasy
Refreshed Lent
Moist Love
Think Took
Bad Humor
Wrinkled Thin
Idiotic Head

Message: Did you ever take home a fish this size? No sir, I throw the little ones back.

Acrostic Puzzle: Synonyms #1 (p. 71)

Defiant Edition
Nasty Sullen
Clutch Thaw
Sofa Sly
Hairy Spirit
Cool Howl
Hop

Message: How can you tell if a school is haunted? If it has school spirit.

Acrostic Puzzle: Synonyms #2 (p. 72)

Hinder Adored
Weighed Ceased
Please Kicks
Notion Stay
Pout Patty
Clean

Message: What candy do kids like to eat on the playground? Recess pieces.

Answer Keys

Acrostic Puzzle:
Synonyms #3 (p. 73)

Bewildered	Rot
Conditions	Choke
Growled	Motto
Feast	Shy
Myths	Home

Message: Why do some kids forget to come to school? They're absent-minded.

Split the Diamond Puzzle:
Scrambled Words #1
(p. 74)
y
to
bug
grim
treat
dreams
jogging
swooping
opponents
obedient
meddles
indeed
picks
trot
ade
et
r
Message: You're a good decoder.

Split the Diamond Puzzle:
Scrambled Words #2
(p. 75)
i
me
sac
duck
Incas
incase
cereals
scissors
upholster
watchful
sunburn
cackle
cacao
bags
ran
in
n
Message: I'm successful again.

Split the Diamond Puzzle:
Scrambled Words #3
(p. 76)
w
or
rag
kilt
hydro
bricks
breathe
smallpox
producing
assorted
assumed
clumsy
rocks
ache
den
as
s
Message: Work yields success.

Split the Diamond Puzzle:
Scrambled Words #4
(p. 77)
i
so
ape
slap
timid
itself
attempt
showered
steamboat
ridicule
science
thanks
remit
hobo
end
do
s
Message: I split the diamonds.

Word Game:
Vocabulary With "TH" Combinations (p. 78)

1. throb	14. tithe
2. there	15. lathe
3. thump	16. month
4. think	17. death
5. theme	18. mouth
6. thorn	19. heath
7. thigh	20. earth
8. thick	21. tooth
9. ether	22. touch
10. other	23. truth
11. paths	24. trash
12. moths	25. teeth
13. bathe	

Word Game:
Vocabulary With "EN" Combinations (p. 79)

1. ensue	14. scent
2. endow	15. blend
3. enjoy	16. often
4. envoy	17. women
5. enemy	18. liven
6. tense	19. risen
7. fence	20. aspen
8. centi	21. reign
9. venom	22. sedan
10. dense	23. deign
11. wrens	24. begin
12. spend	25. seven
13. agent	

Word Game:
Vocabulary With "SP" Combinations (p. 80)

1. spend	14. soppy
2. spite	15. super
3. speed	16. clasp
4. sport	17. grasp
5. space	18. wasps
6. shops	19. rasps
7. shape	20. sloop
8. slope	21. steep
9. snips	22. swamp
10. steps	23. scrap
11. sepal	24. sharp
12. sappy	25. sleep
13. sapid	

Word Game:
Vocabulary With "LE" Combinations (p. 81)

1. lethal	14. relent
2. ledges	15. alleys
3. levers	16. giggle
4. letter	17. hassle
5. leader	18. needle
6. clever	19. icicle
7. please	20. handle
8. sleepy	21. league
9. sleeve	22. lassie
10. pledge	23. linage
11. select	24. little
12. inlets	25. locate
13. allege	